GOOD NEWS POETRY

GOOD NEWS POETRY

NOEL R TOWNS

Published by Noel R Towns
noel.towns@gmail.com

First published 2020

Scripture quotations are from the Holy Bible, New International Version (NIV) unless stated otherwise.

A catalogue record for this book is available from the National Library of Australia

ISBN 978 0 6488955 0 3 (pbk)

Cover designed by Sketchbook
Typeset by Helen Christie
Printed by Ingram Spark

CONTENTS

DEDICATION AND THANKS

I would like to dedicate this book to Christina, my wife, our nine beautiful children, our twenty-six grand-children and our two great grand-children. I pray for them all constantly.

This book is also dedicated to my ninety year old mother, my eight siblings and all of their respective families that add up to over one hundred people. Imagine when we all get together. We need to hire a church building.

I also wish to acknowledge all those who have come on this journey with me. It started out as a pleasurable hobby and ended up a full blown book.

I would like to thank my proof readers; Graeme Erb, Ros Atkinson and Jenny Johnston. They have each put in many hours correcting my grammar and, at times, to help with a more natural flow, have made helpful suggestions with regard to rhyme, rhythm and word choice.

I would like to thank my nephew Gary Wright, who took my raw ideas for the book cover and turned them into a creative and dramatic finished product, with which I am most pleased.

And finally, Helen Christie, who typeset the book and gave it the finishing touches it needed to become more readable.

To all these people I say a big thank you. It is the combination of talents that go into a work like this that allow it to have maximum impact on the reader.

FOREWORD

It would have really stretched my imagination if, when I first met Noel nearly fifty-five years ago, I had been told that one day he would write a book of poetry. My first memory of Noel and his large family was when they filed into our little church one Sunday morning, occupying two rows of seats. Their coming considerably added to the number in our congregation. His family fit in well with us and lifelong friendships began at that time. Noel inherited his family's talent for singing and he was often up the front strumming his guitar, singing with his own unique style.

Tenacity, determination and persistence are three character traits that have stood Noel in good stead throughout his life. I well remember celebrating his last night of singleness before his wedding to Christina. His Riverside friends decided that a dip in the icy waters of the North Esk River, near Launceston, would be an appropriate manner in which to celebrate the occasion of his marriage the next day. Noel was obviously no match in size for several of those friends but I have never seen anyone fight so tenaciously and with such determination to avoid their inevitable fate. I feared that Christina, his beautiful bride, would be met next day at the altar by a husband sporting a black eye, missing teeth or worse. After an incredible struggle, Noel received the dunking he had so desperately tried to avoid without any obvious collateral damage to his body.

Noel's first book, *Back From the Other Side*, details how his determination, persistence and tenacious character have enabled him to achieve what he has, both in his personal and family life, as well as in business. Noel would freely acknowledge though that, ultimately, it was his unswerving personal faith in Jesus Christ and God's good hand upon him that have enabled him to achieve all that he has. It has been special to reconnect with Noel and Christina in recent years as they have settled into retirement and, once again, attend our church in Riverside.

When Noel and I meet together, whether it be for a coffee or at church, I come away encouraged by something Noel has learnt from his Bible, from the latest book that he has read or from some podcast he has listened to. Often I am challenged by his genuine desire that every member of his family, his friends and daily contacts come to know and experience the same authentic relationship that he enjoys with his Lord and Saviour, Jesus Christ.

I was somewhat surprised one day when Noel mentioned that he was writing poems in his spare time. As he sent me several to read, I understood why he had started writing poetry. Poetry is about life and differs from other forms of writing in that it expresses ideas and feelings with a greater intensity. Noel has, through his poems, expressed his intense and passionate desire that we as readers might come to understand matters dear to his heart. A careful reading of each poem will give a better understanding of many of the questions we may have with regard to the Bible and the ultimate issues of life; this present one and the one to come. Applying their message to our lives will make an eternal difference.

Graeme L. Erb
July 1st, 2020

PREFACE

On the 30th August, 2016, I suffered a health event which resulted in me dying for forty-five minutes. I lost about seven or eight days and woke up in ICU with nurses and doctors telling me that I was a miracle.

Sometime over those few days, I received a message from God which I later recounted in a book titled, *Back From the Other Side*. The only things I can recall from that time, are the message I received and the prayer that I prayed, "Lord I am ready to come, but I am also ready to stay." The fact that I have written this book of poems tells you that I survived. For some reason, for the time being, God wanted me to stay.

I don't believe that we are meant to be here to just survive, take up space and breathe air. I believe God has a purpose for each of us. So I have been seeing what new things have unfolded in my life since leaving hospital in 2016.

One of the things that has occurred is that God has re-kindled a latent passion in me. When I was much younger, I used to write songs. Later on when I became busy with raising a family and working to provide for them, this passion laid dormant in me for many years.

My wife and I like to take walks as part of our health regime and, as we do, I often hear rhymes forming in my mind. When I return home, I quickly write them down in case I forget them. Many of the poems in this book started from a seed which began while I was walking and then grew into a full blown poem later on.

The theme running through these poems is, in my view, the most important good news story that can ever be told. That is the message of the Gospel – that we are all sinners, that there is a penalty for our sin, Jesus Christ paid that penalty on our behalf and salvation is available to everyone who genuinely calls upon the name of the Lord (Romans 10:13).

If we will turn from doing life our own way to doing life His way (Repentance), through faith in Him and by His grace, we can be saved (Eph. 2:8). The message of the Gospel is foolishness to the human mind and can only be spiritually discerned. If we look to do life God's way with the help of the Holy Spirit, we will enter into an abundant, satisfying life which He promises for each of us (John 10:10).

Sharing this message often opens one up to ridicule. But if reading this book of poems results in one soul entering into the Kingdom of Heaven, this work is worthwhile and ridicule is a small price to pay.

These poems are perhaps different to any that you have read. They are an attempt to write the Scriptures into poetry. You will note that many Scripture references are included at the end of each poem. This is so you can look up the Bible references to ascertain if the message portrayed, accurately reflects the Scriptural thought. Any sermon we hear, devotional book we read or biblical information we obtain from any other source, should always be viewed through the lens or prism of Scripture.

You will find that many of these poems are powerful and enter deep into the psyche and heart of the reader. This is not due to "my words" but the power that comes from "His Word," the Bible.

Hebrews 4:12–13 says,

"For the Word of God is living and active. Sharper than any double edged sword, it penetrates even dividing soul and spirit, joints and marrow; it judges the thoughts and attitude of the heart. Nothing in all creation is hidden from God's sight. Everything is uncovered and laid bare before the eyes of Him to whom we must give account."

This means that God's Word is like no other writing in the history of the world. It is living, Spirit breathed (2 Tim. 3:16) and the person of the Holy Spirit teaches and ministers to us while we read it (John 14:25–26).

But many try to read God's Word and don't understand it. That is why the Bible teaches that if we seek Him, we will find Him (Matt. 7:7–8). If you make a genuine attempt to seek the Lord, the Bible says we will find Him. The Holy Spirit opens up our blind eyes and allows us to understand what is written in His Word.

You may also note that there are fifty-two poems which allows the reader, if they so desire, to meditate on one poem per week for an entire year. That is to use the poems as a type of weekly devotional. Some poems contain a single theme or thought for the reader to meditate upon. Others are more theological in nature and draw on several parts of Scripture. At this point however, I must issue a word of caution. These poems were never intended to replace Scripture. If by reading them however, a hunger and thirst for God's Word is kindled, then they have served a higher and better purpose.

The other point I would like to make about these poems is that they first minister to me before they minister to you. Ask any Pastor who prepares a sermon to share with their church members. The Word of God is just as applicable to the Pastor as it is to their congregation.

I have seen elements of myself in many of the poems I have written. I think God has used His words to challenge my own life first before He uses them to challenge your life. We can all take God for granted when times are good, but find ourselves upon our knees when we are desperate. God wants us to be desperate for Him always, in both good and bad times. He must be the one for whom we thirst and He is the only one who can quench our thirst. He is the Living Water and Bread of life. Only He satisfies our yearnings.

If you know me personally and see yourself in any of these poems, please be aware that they are about none of us and yet all of us at the same time. In other words, I did not have particular people in mind as I wrote these poems. But I do see myself in most of them and you may find you see elements or yourself in them as well.

Finally, when writing poems, the writer is usually concerned with the issues of the rhythm and the rhyme. But more importantly, in my view, is that the poem tells a compelling story. I may have erred in getting the rhythm and the rhyme exactly right on some occasions, but I pray I have not erred in presenting the Gospel story accurately (but you can make that judgement for yourself).

GOOD NEWS POETRY

A BABY BORN

A tiny miracle knit together in its mother's womb,
More intricate than a flower in the splendour of full bloom.
Perfect little feet and hands, sweet fingers and cute toes.
Only once we've had a child, do we *really* know.

An overflowing heart of joy, we'll never be the same.
A love we've never felt before, but hope we will again.
We have such lofty hopes for this precious baby child,
That they'll grow up fit and well, with character undefiled.

Those tiny little feet will make large footprints on our heart.
We can't imagine how we could ever be apart.
We carefully watch their progress, hearts filled with pure delight.
Our baby can do nothing wrong and everything just right.

We hear their gurgles and their coos, each precious baby sound,
Invading us with pleasure and causing hearts to pound.
We see them first roll over, and then they start to crawl,
And finally they try to walk, while hoping not to fall.

In the middle of the night, we wake up to their cry,
Responding to their call and with little sleep get by.
A world with lots of bad things, we would change them if we could,
But we look into our baby's eyes and everything is good.

Forty weeks, a little less, it takes this miracle to form,
Yet the bond of love is instant the day that they are born.
Each little life's a miracle, created just to be,
The miracle of you, and the miracle of me.

Every person who's created, every baby that is born,
Is like a new day ushered in at breaking of the dawn.
Bringing the magic of sunshine and light for you and me,
They are full of possibilities of all that they might be.

We have such dreams and hopes for our baby born,
Yet many times throughout their lives our hearts may well be torn.
But the constant love we have for them will never pass away.
For hope-filled lives and protection, we will always pray.

---

1 Sam. 1: 27–28, Psalm 127:3, 139: 13–14. Eccl. 11:5, Isaiah 44:24, 49:15,
Matt. 18:10, 19:14, Mark 10:16, John 16:21, 1 Pet.2:2.

A FATHER'S LOVE

There was a time, long, long ago,
When God, upon us, His Love did bestow.
And the creatures too, which He had made …
All His creation, Him rightly obeyed.

Adam and Eve were happy in the garden.
They hadn't sinned, so needed no pardon.
In His own image, they both had been made.
God walked with them, they were unafraid.

Their Heavenly Father gave Adam a rule.
Confusion about it, Satan later would fuel.
"Of the trees in the garden, you are free to eat.
There's plenty of fruit, the garden's replete.

But the tree of the knowledge of evil and good,
Don't ever be tempted to eat for your food.
I know it's most pleasing to your eye,
But the day that you eat it, you surely will die."

Not long after, the snake tempted Eve,
With smooth words, he set out, her to deceive.
"What was it God told you on that day?
To not taste of any tree, did He say?"

Eve gave the serpent her forthright reply.
"Fruit from all of the trees, we're able to try.
Excepting the middle one, we must comply.
God said, 'If you eat it or touch it, you'll die'."

Satan whispered to Eve, "You will not surely die.
God knows if you eat, it will open your eyes.
You will be like Him, knowing evil and good.
It also gives wisdom, and is pleasant for food."

Eve saw it was indeed good to the eye.
She ate it and gave some to Adam to try.
Then, sin in their mortal bodies did reign.
Communion with God would not be the same.

Now the friendship they had with God was broken.
They did not obey the word He had spoken.
So God drove them out from the garden that day.
And the penalty for sin would have to be paid.

While God really wanted their bond be restored,
Adam and Eve's sin could not be ignored.
The Father's heart was now torn asunder,
But it made Him reveal an amazing wonder.

At the right time, God planned Jesus to send.   1
Love and Justice working in perfect blend.
His Justice demanded punishment for sin.   2
His love meant the penalty He took upon Him.   3

It's as though I was made to sit in the dock.
The case brought against me, solid as a rock.   4
I know that I'm guilty … without even a shock,
The jail door slams, the key turns in the lock!

Suppose the sentence was the whip's cruel lash,
But removing his shirt, the Judge bares his own back.
And there makes his stand for all to see.
Taking the punishment meant for me.

And our Heavenly Father is just like that Judge.
He blots out our sin, not leaving a smudge. 5
In Christ's own body, He bore on the tree, 6
The penalty for sin, owed by both you and me.

I picture my Father's love for me, 7
As he sits 'His child' upon His knee.
The pleasure and joy I can bring to His heart, 8
As a family member His blessings impart.

Sometimes when we're tempted to run away, wild,
He gently reminds us we are always His child. 9
And at times when His word we fail to obey,
He longs to see us drop to our knees, and pray.

He so wants to forgive, to restore us again, 10
To heal all our troubles and share in our pain. 11
The best for His children he desires to see,
If we turn back to Him, His delight we will be. 12

Gen. Chs. 2 and 3. 1. Gal. 4:4–5. 2. Rom. 3:25–26. 3. 1 Peter 2:24. 4. Rom. 3:23.
5. Isaiah 43:25. 6. 1 Pet. 2:24. 7. 2 Cor. 6:18. 8. Zeph. 3:17. 9. John 1:12, Rom. 8:16.
10. 1 John 1:9, Col. 1:13–14. 11. 2 Cor. 1:4. 12. Ps. 149:4.

A LAND OF GOLD

From humble beginnings, into this world you came.
Your dreams only small, you weren't destined for fame.
Your house, a simple hut, with mud and cow dung walls,
Too thin to deaden any sounds of animals' night-time calls.
You've heard of houses far away that would keep out the cold,
And could only dream of living there, in the land of gold.

Your belly always ached, you longed to fill it up with food,
Of the tough meat once a day, that your mother always stewed.
You had only one set of clothes, tattered and torn.
And for a very long time, the same ones you'd worn.
Too poor to be embarrassed, you were a sight to behold,
But all of this would surely change, in the land of gold.

You never had any money, education could not afford.
In any case there were no jobs, your hard work would reward.
And then your mother was unwell and could no longer work.
Your father left her long ago, responsibility he shirked.
But there was a place in the world, of which you'd been told,
Where fortunes would all turn around, in the land of gold.

You were too young to work, or a meagre job to find.
Your only hope was that the neighbours to you would be kind.
Your mother's health had worsened and, sadly, she died.
You were now completely alone, and to your God you cried.
If only your life could change, from your miseries untold.
Yes, all your troubles would be over, in the land of gold.

Then some people came into your life, you could hardly believe.
They wanted you to join their family, and your pain relieve.
You did not expect God to answer your cry to Him so soon.
He sent them at the very time your life was in total ruin.
You just couldn't take it in, especially when you were told.
They had travelled from far away, from that land of gold.

When you left your homeland, with sadness you did go.
The land where you were going, you didn't really know.
But you were also very excited, and you could hardly wait,
To travel to the land of gold, that God had made your fate.
And your new family told you, "You are welcome to the fold."
At last you would fulfil your dream, in that land of gold.

Before you arrived there, you couldn't believe your eyes.
You had often seen those planes that flew above you in the skies.
But to actually be in one, and look down on the earth below,
Had only been a pipe dream you were sure you'd never know.
You loved your nice new family, tightly to them you'd hold.
You would never want to go away, from that land of gold.

Suddenly you were there, seeing sights you'd never seen.
And you would go to many places, you had never been.
Smells were unfamiliar, strange language and new sounds.
Possibilities everywhere, your excitement knew no bounds.
When you look back to that time, you couldn't have foretold.
How your life was about to change, in that land of gold.

And so your stomach no longer suffered with hunger and with pain.
You wondered would you ever know that hunger again.
And now you're always sleeping, in a warm and cosy bed.
You have so many clothes now, some of them you need to shed.
It did not take very long here to be squeezed into its mould.
It's hard to remember not living in this land of gold.

You now have education, many things you have learned.
You enjoy work and saved much money that you've earned.
There's no need now to ask God for help, like you used to pray,
To supply you with all your needs, for each and every day.
You have most things you want and have become very bold.
And now there's no real need for God, in this land of gold.

You now have all the gadgets that money can possibly buy.
Rarely thinking of your homeland, and when you said goodbye.
Your mother's long forgotten, as well as Jesus Christ your Lord.
How often you used to pray to Him and love to obey His Word.
Though you now, well and truly, have a very strong foothold.
You know that something's missing, in this 'lovely' land of gold.

Deut. 4:9–14, Ch. 6, Ch. 8.

A NEW COVENANT

In history past, our God made a promise to the Jews,   1
To guide and protect them, if Him they were to choose.
"If you decide to follow Me, I'll promise you this day,
An everlasting covenant, if my laws you will obey."

So all the land of Israel God guaranteed to give,
Through Abraham, a People Great would forever live.
His treasured possession, a Holy Nation it would be,
"These blessings are yours," God said, "if you just follow Me."

God said, "Moses build a tabernacle, with an inner sanctuary."   2
On Mt Sinai's pattern, a copy of Heaven it would be.
A place where only the High Priest was allowed come,   3
And only God could dwell, the priest, a shadow of His Son.   4

God promised His people He would pardon all their sin,   5
If sacrifices brought were offered by the priest, to Him.
Animals unblemished, upon the altar laid,   6
Their spilt blood an offering for sin, atonement made.   7

The High priest could only enter there but once a year,   8
In the Holy of Holies before God's presence to appear.
He sprinkled the blood sacrifice for his own sin first,   9
Reparation now was made, to cover Adam's curse.   10

But God found fault with the old covenant He'd made.   11
Sacrifices brought no pleasure, for sin was not allayed.   12
The blood of bulls and goats could never cover sin.   13
A better covenant He had in mind, the old He would rescind.   14

If the old one still could stand, a new one would not be sought,   15
So in Christ a spotless sacrifice, a better covenant was wrought.   16
By His death, a one-time sacrifice for sin was made for all.   17
No other offering would suffice, or sin's wages would forestall.   18

Without shedding of the blood, there's no forgiveness for our sin.   19
Christ not only shed His blood, but to Heaven entered in.   20
This was indeed the true one, unlike a man-made sanctuary.
He entered God's very presence, on behalf of you and me.

God puts His law into our mind and writes it on our hearts.   21
He declares we are His people, from Him never to depart.   22
He says we'll really know Him, and we can be very sure,   23
He forgives us all our wickedness, remembers our sin no more.   24

When Jesus cried, "It's finished," and breathed His one last breath,   25
He dropped His head, gave up His soul, and submitted unto death.
An amazing and symbolic sign occurred, for all to see,   26
The temple curtain tore in two, a miracle could only be.

God took away this partition, the hostile dividing wall,   27
Abolishing with His flesh, the commandments one and all.
With confidence we can come now, receive mercy and God's grace.   28
For Jesus sits at God's right hand in this Most Holy Place.   29

So we come to God more boldly and directly can approach.   30
Into the Holy of Holies without fear we might encroach.
But we must always come to Him in meek humility,
Only through our Saviour, in God's presence can we be.

In His presence we couldn't stand, separated by our sin.   31
But through imputed righteousness we now can enter in,
To stand before His Throne, without arrogance, and bold.
It's only through Christ Jesus, that God's glory we behold.

---

1. Gen. Ch. 15, 16. 2. Ex. Ch. 25. 3. Heb. 9:7, Lev. Ch. 16. 4. Heb. 8:5. 5. Lev. 4:20.
6. Lev 22:17–25. 7. Lev 4:32. 8. Heb. 9:7, Lev. 16:2-34. 9. Heb. 5:3. 10. Lev. 16:6.
11. Heb. 8:8. 12. Isaiah 1:11, Heb. 10:6–8. 13. Heb. 10:4. 14. Heb. 8:8–9. 15. Heb. 8:7.
16. Heb. 8:6. 17. Rom. 6:10, Heb. 9:26, 10:10 18. Heb. 10:26–27, Rom 6:23.
19. Heb. 9:22. 20. Heb. 9:24. 21. Heb. 8:10, 10:16. 22. John 10:28–30. 23. Heb. 8:10.
24. Heb. 10:17. 25. John 19:30. 26. Matt. 27:51. 27. Eph. 2:14–15. 28. Heb. 4:16.
29. Heb. 8:1, 10:12. 30. Heb. 4:16. 31. Heb. 1:13, Ps. 5:4–5.

A PRAYER OF WORSHIP

My most loving and gracious Father,
Beside you my God there is no other.
Into your most Holy presence I come,
Because of the victory on the cross Jesus won.
Thank you Jesus for dying there for me,
For In God's presence I can now be.
So, I come to You now in Jesus' Name.
I humbly worship you my Lord again.

You are maker of heaven and earth.
Mighty works displayed in the universe.
Your knowledge, God, knows no bounds.
No other compares or can ever be found.
So, to You my Father I commit my soul,
Resting in the knowledge that You're in control.
So, I come to You now in Jesus' Name.
I gladly worship you my Lord again.

How I long for You Father each day.
You give me purpose along the way.
What would my life without you be?
I would be unsure of my final destiny.
Maybe looking ahead to death in fear,
With no future hope of You being near.
So, I come to You now in Jesus' Name.
I thankfully worship you my Lord again.

In all places at one time You can be.
How immense is Your glory and majesty.
So how is it that You could possibly be,
Desiring to have a relationship with me?
One day in your presence my dear Lord,
Is better than all this world can afford.
So, I come to You now in Jesus' Name.
Fall down to worship you my Lord again.

I ask You dear Lord to forgive my sin.
Give your Spirit's power for me to win.
For the battle against evil every day.
Supernatural power from you I pray.
Grace to forgive sisters and brothers,
Who sin against me and offend others.
So, I come to You now in Jesus' Name.
I gratefully worship you my Lord again.

You're the Bread of Life my soul to fill.
And I know you are God when I am still.
My thirsty soul's yearning You satisfy.
For to live is Christ, it's my gain to die.
May my daily needs by You be supplied.
But more importantly in me to abide.
So, in His name I come to You again.
I joyfully worship you my Lord. Amen.

A SOUL LIKE YOU AND ME

There this young girl stood in her modest garb.
To look upon this five year old was really very hard.
An extended, outstretched hand so small and brown.
Desperate and dishevelled while begging she was found.
"Give me shilling," was her cry – an oft' repeated phrase.
I felt my heart begin to bleed, the sight I can't erase.
"Do not give to her," they said, "her owners you may feed."
But this beautiful child has a soul, just like you and me.

I pushed away well-meant advice and money did I sneak,
To this dearest little one who to me did plead and seek.
Once her quest was satisfied, the fulfilment of her need,
She turned away in happiness and skipped away with glee.
Worth much more than what I gave was the pleasure on her face.
I felt the heart of Jesus there to comfort and embrace.
He once again reminded me, the truth He let me see.
This one He loves has a soul, just like you and me

Another day, another scene our senses would assault.
My pre-conceived reality and notions took a jolt.
Standing before us, another impoverished little girl.
She had no standing or value in our indifferent world.
She was even more desperate in filthy rags she stood.
I would pick her up and take her home, if only I could.
Matted hair and runny nose, unembarrassed for us to see.
A precious pearl who has a soul, just like you and me.

We next visited a slum, with many children there,
So excited to meet us, singing hymns with us to share.
And why such happy, smiling faces in the midst of poverty?
We are told if they eat today, from our tip their meal will be.
I silently call out to my Lord, to ask the reason why.
I cannot take it anymore, succumb, break down and cry.
How often can emotions crack? How heart-broken can one be?
I'm reminded that they all have souls, just like you and me.

For another confrontation, how could we possibly prepare?
A home where children, missing limbs, were abandoned there.
Longing to hold strangers' hands that would not let them go.
Desperate for one to really care, and for their love to know.
It's so hard to see these children, raw emotions running high.
But I'm able now to gain control, and manage not to cry.
My thoughts turn again to home, where we live in luxury,
While those before us have a soul, just like you and me.

Then there was a desperate mother, trying her life to end.
She was pregnant with a child, who on her would depend.
But this child's life was precious, and destined to be spared.
Her mother found help from a place where God's great love was shared.
It came to pass that "Eyerus," a precious baby girl was born.
She came into a broken world, a world that was war-torn.
But Eyerus and her mother thrived despite their poverty.
Jesus loving and blessing their souls, just like you and me.

There are lots of other stories, I could tell so many more.
Countless people we have met, lessons learned from the poor.
Causing confronting questions to be raised in my mind.
The answers are most difficult and very hard to find.
Why so materially impoverished, yet spiritually alive?
In contrast we are spiritually poor, while materially we thrive.
And if our world were to crumble, would we contented be,
Sharing with those who have a soul, just like you and me?

And I still ponder questions, run them over in my mind.
I keep searching for answers, if I seek I may well find.
Why are they so generous, always want to share and give;
Radiating such joy and happiness, when in poverty they live?
Why is it that I was born so rich in comparison to them?
It cannot be that I'm worth more, or from my merit stem.
Why do we so often ignore others' lives of misery?
When Jesus loves all with a soul, just like you and me?

Prov. 19:17. Matt. 19:13–14. Mark 9:36–37. James 2:14–16. 1 John 3:16–18.

AN ANSWER TO WHY WE SUFFER

With all of life's problems, mankind seeks to solve.
This is perhaps the greatest, in our minds to resolve.
And possibly it's foolish, in a poem so short.
Attempting an explanation, and to human logic resort.

To say, "an answer" not "the answer," gives a clue.
This quest provides a mystery, we all seek to construe.
No answer can ever be complete, or fully explain.
Why suffering in the world exists, and why we feel pain.

And if I'm truly honest, this question's often asked by me.
Why doesn't God intervene, with all the suffering that He sees?
For many innocent children, He sees them starve and die.
Again, I come before my God, and ask the question, why.

Maybe I'll get an answer, when I meet God, face to face.
Though I carry this great burden, He still saved me by His grace.
So, to explain this dilemma, my attempt may be poor.
Perhaps it may be helpful, for other questions to explore.

Instead of asking "why" maybe ask "when" or "where."
Where did it come from? When of suffering were we aware?
It happened in the garden, when man chose to rebel.
Adam and Eve left Eden, no longer there to dwell.

God withdrew His provision, and protection from harm.
Now fending for themselves, there was real cause for alarm.
God said thorns and thistles, would come from the soil.
And man would eat his food, through sweat and painful toil.

He said pain would increase, when women give birth.
That mankind made from the dust, would return to earth.
Answering the "when" and "where" of pain, doesn't always help.
When we ourselves do suffer and by us the pain is felt.

It may not be our concern to know why it came to be,
Because the fact that we are suffering is our present reality.
Reasons for pain we can suggest and no doubt some are true.
Neat answers cannot soothe the pain when faced by me and you.

We know suffering when we see it, though it's hard to define.
We all feel some pain or loss, it can happen any time.
Some say suffering wouldn't be, if a God really does exist.
But when they suffer pain, it's at Him they shake their fist.   2

If there really was no God, then who would they then blame?
And if the world was Godless, mankind would suffer the same.
Human beings may not understand why suffering does exist.
But we know it isn't optional, it is always in our midst.

Suffering's answer is like a wound, which has refused to heal.
While our faith it does challenge, our faith helps with it to deal.
God didn't forever leave Adam's race for themselves to fend.   3
He sent Christ to suffer on a cross and their bond to mend.   4

No Heavenly host did He bring, but saved us from within.   5
In His own body Christ suffered all the pain caused by our sin.   6
When He cried, "My God, My God, why have you forsaken me?"   7
He knew the very depths of pain, as to God He made His plea.

God is in the midst of suffering and in our pain He shares. 8

Healed by the Lord's stripes, from sin's wages, us He spares. 9

Why we suffer we can't explain, but suffering is a fact.

Our challenge is to cope with pain and still keep our faith intact. 10

Christ left us with an example to be followed by you and me. 11

Just as He suffered in His flesh, Jesus to people we can be. 12

Being there for others, helping the poor their needs to meet. 13

And everywhere we go, we can be Jesus' hands and feet. 14

---

1. Gen. Ch. 3. 2. Job 15:25. 3. 2 Tim. 1:12. 4. Rom. 5:10. 5. Matt. 26:53. 6. 1 Pet. 2:24.
7. Matt. 27:46. 8. 2 Cor. 1:5. 9. Isaiah 53:5, Rom. 6:23. 10. Job 13:15, Ps. 23:4.
11. 1 Pet. 2:21. 12. Rom. 12:15. 13. 2 Cor. 1:3–4, James 1:27. 14. Mark 10:45, John 13:14.

AS OFTEN AS YOU DO THIS

On the first day of the Feast of Unleavened Bread,
Jesus, aware His blood was soon to be shed,
Told His disciples to go to Jerusalem,
To prepare a Passover feast to eat with them.

He said, "Once you arrive, a man you will meet.
He will show you a room where we all can eat."
So the room was found and was duly prepared.
And a meal with His disciples, Jesus then shared.

His appointed time was drawing ever near.
That He would suffer, to Him was very clear.
Later at the table, where they happened to be,
Jesus said, "One of you here, will betray me."

The one named Judas said, "Surely not I?"
"Yes, you're the betrayer," was the Lord's reply.
The Pharisees, wanting to end Jesus' life,
Secretly with Judas, did plot and connive.

"What you're going to do, do quickly," He said.
Judas left after Jesus gave him some bread.
Jesus was aware His time would soon come,
And that after His death, victory would be won.

Of course Jesus knew He would rise from the dead,
But first there would be much suffering ahead.
So, while they ate, He picked up some bread,
Gave thanks, broke it and to His disciples said,

"This bread is my Body, it is broken for you.
Take it and eat it and as often as you do,
Think of my life, I am giving for thee,
And take it always, in remembrance of me."

In the very same way He took a cup of wine.
Reminded them again that each and every time,
They drank from the cup, to remember Him by,
It symbolized the blood, He would pour out, and die.

The Apostle Paul's words still come to mind,
Centuries later, when we ourselves find,
We too remember what Jesus has done,
And our Heavenly Father, who gave us His son.

He said Jesus' blood was poured out for many,
A new covenant, now available to any,
Who for pardon of sins, call upon His Name.
The Lord's death until He returns, we proclaim.

Matt 26:26–27, Mark 14:22–24, Luke 22:19–20, 1 Cor. 11:23–26.

BODY, SOUL AND SPIRIT

Does the soul have a body, or the body have a soul?
Is there body, soul and spirit, for a person to be whole?
These questions we may ponder, which are not so often clear.
Will soul and spirit live eternal and just the body disappear?

We know we have a body, which houses our brain.
And when the body dies, it goes back to dust again.
But are thoughts gone forever, nothing to survive?
Only memories others have of us, when we were once alive?

It's said that thoughts are chemical reactions in the brain.
But are thoughts and feelings, no-where else to be contained?
Are there parts of our being which help to play a role?
Does a mind outside the body, have a home within the soul?

If we give our body to science, after we have passed.
No soul can a scalpel find, for death it does outlast.
Where can we find answers, where the truth to find?
Does the Bible have solutions, to satisfy our mind?

The soul leaves your body on the day that you will die.
The body sees decay, which to the soul does not apply.
It goes on to live for ever, survives for all eternity.
An appointment with our Maker, awaits both you and me.

The spirit is that part of us which communes with our God.
It's quickened when we respond to the Holy Spirit's prod.
For when our soul is born again, our spirit comes alive.
His Spirit witnesses with our own, which He does revive.

So while soul and spirit are living in this earthly tent,   10
God's Holy Spirit with your spirit pleads, of sin to repent.   11
This means a change of mind about doing life yourself.
Jesus said the poor in spirit, will receive Heavenly wealth.   12

When the scales are lifted, from the blind eyes of our hearts,   13
We finally see and understand, true wisdom God imparts.   14
But when we see through the prism of a human mind,
Our reasoning is limited, because our souls are blind.   15

Do I need to understand all of God, to believe?
Or simply trust in Him, to know and to receive?
For when we put our faith in Him, His Spirit inside us lives.   16
And then we have His Spirit's mind, which to us He freely gives.   17

Salvation's message is so foolish to the human mind.   18
It's spiritually understood, so with His Spirit we can find.   19
When finally our foolish hearts in surrender to Him be,
Our spiritual eyes are opened and we can plainly see.

We then make our earthly tent, the Holy Spirit's home,   20
And from that day onwards, we'll never be alone.   21
Love, joy, peace and other fruits the Spirit will employ.   22
Kindness, gentleness, self-control will be ours to enjoy.

---

1. Hebrews 4:12, 1 Thess. 5:23. 2. Ecclesiastes 12:7. 3. Ps. 30:12, 86:12.
4. Gen 35:18 (ESV) Luke 12:20 (KJV). 5. Ps. 30:12, 86:12. 6. Hebrews 9:27.
7. Eph. 2:1–5. 8. John 3:5–6, 1 Cor. 15:22. 9. Rom. 8:16, 2 Tim. 4:22.
10. 2 Cor. 5:1. 11. John 16:8. 12. Deut. 4:29, Matt. 5:3. 13. Rom. 1:21, Eph. 4:18.
14. Eph. 1:17. 15. 1 Cor. 2:13. 16. 1 Cor. 6:17. 17. 1 Cor. 2:11–12. 18. 1 Cor. 1:18.
19. Job 32:8, 1 Cor. 2:14. 20. 1 Cor. 6:19. 21. John 14:15. 22. Gal. 5:22.

CAST THE FIRST STONE

People gathered round Him, in the temple court.
Jesus sat among them, as the people He taught.
And the teachers of the Law, then to Jesus brought.
A woman who, they said, in adultery was caught.

So before the group, she was forced to stand;
A way to trap Jesus, had been carefully planned.
They said, "In the Law of Moses, for this woman's sin,
She should be stoned to death," her situation looking grim.

"What do you say?" An attempt to publicly expose,
And to silence Jesus, who a threat to them did pose.
A plan to embarrass Him and His entrapment sought,
But what about the man who was also in adultery caught?

It appears a well thought out plan was about to unfold.
Though the woman was guilty, a guilty man too was involved.
But the teachers of the law had no interest in the man.
Bringing him before the crowd would not suit their plan.

To favour her release, Jesus would seem to break the Law.
If He said, "Execute her," He would break it even more.
If Jesus advocated this, then Him they would accuse.
Religious execution rights had been taken from the Jews.

His response was unexpected, for He simply just bent down.
Then with His finger, He began to write upon the ground.
Jesus ignored the accusers, as if He had not heard.
He kept writing in the sand and didn't say a word.

There is much speculation on what Jesus actually wrote.
Was He stalling for extra time, or simply from the Law did quote?
The Jews kept asking questions. They aimed them straight at Him.
Not caring for true righteousness, or concerned with their own sin.

Jesus was gracious to the woman, but didn't want to be unjust.
Not wishing to break the Law, but to show her love He must.
So, when He straightened up, this is what He said to them,
"The first one to throw a stone can be anyone without sin."

One by one they left, as again He wrote upon the ground.
From the oldest to the youngest, until no-one there was found.
And as Jesus began to straighten up, He then became aware,
That only He and the woman were now left standing there.

Jesus said, "Woman, where are those accusers of yours?
Does not a one condemn you?" She said, "No-one, Lord."
To exercise His love and grace, but not her sin ignore,
He said, "Neither do I condemn you, go and sin no more."

There is a common sin of ours, which was exposed by Him.
An awful desire to punish others, while ignoring our own sin.
Jesus' life always showed how each of us should live.
He avoided power to condemn, by His power we forgive.

John 8:1–11.

CONTENTMENT

She was a dear old lady, a story written on her face.
Every wrinkled line showed forth a message of God's grace.
It's not that life was easy, she was a struggling old soul. 1
For all her hardship, she lived a life, which was complete and whole. 2

For she long ago learned secrets, which few of us do learn.
She turned her back on sin, knew what wage sins would earn. 3
Very little seemed to trouble this happy, wise, old soul. 4
She didn't share her own trials, but did others in grief console. 5

She had no worldly wealth, but what she had she valued more. 6
It mattered not one bit to her, she was materially poor. 7
She knew the secret of contentment, revelation most profound. 8
You almost felt, in her presence, you stood on holy ground.

Her mind not set on earthly treasure, or seeking its reward, 9
Her sight was set much higher on the presence of her Lord. 10
What was inside her heart would shine forth loud and clear. 11
No-one could ruffle her feathers, as Jesus was so near. 12

Jesus said to shine our light, so the Father, men would praise. 13
Not to hide it, put it on a stand, the darkness to erase.
This dear lady, a fine example, she was always looking forward, 14
Without a hint of complaint, seeing ahead to Heaven's reward.

And it was so very sad, when from this life she finally passed.
Yes, sad for us but not for her, now in His presence at last. 15
So few people who pass through life, live it with such joy,
Whose hearts, like hers, are Spirit-filled, and who His fruits employ. 16

---

1. Matt. 16:24. 2. John 10:10. 3. Rom. 6:23. 4. Gal. 5:22. 5. 2 Cor. 1:4. 6. 1 Pet. 1:7.
7. Ps. 140:12, Isaiah 61:1. 8. Phil 4:11–13. 9. Col. 3:2. 10. Heb. 12:2. 11. Matt. 5:14.
12. Gal 5:22. 13. Matt. 5:15–16. 14. Heb. 12:2. 15. Phil 1:21. 16. Gal. 5:22.

CORDS OF LOVE

He was born in a stable in the town of Bethlehem,   1
Grew in stature and favour with both God and men.   2
Yet He died at the hands of the ones He dearly loved,   3
And He was forsaken by man and God above.

"If you be the son of God," was their mocking cry,
"Come down and save yourself," but they knew not why.
Jesus could not come down as He shed his blood.
The nails could not hold Him, He was bound with cords of love.

He was laid in a sepulchre, a stone rolled to the door.
The Pharisees were satisfied, they sealed the entrance sure.
But death had no victory and Jesus rose again.
Appeared to His disciples and now lives in hearts of men.   4

"If you be the son of God," was their mocking cry,
"Come down, save yourself," but they knew not why.
Jesus could not come down as He shed his blood.
The nails could not hold Him, He was bound with cords of love.

Matthew Chs. 27 and 28. 1. Matt. 2:5–6. 2. Luke 2:52. 3. John 3:16. 4. John 14:17.

DID JESUS DIE ?

The fact that He lived is historically true.
But when Jesus died for me and you,
Was He actually dead, as reputed to be?
Or did He survive, His death on the tree?

If we were to fully examine this case,
Any doubts that He died, we could surely erase.
What proof would we offer that He really died?
Not just appeared to, and then later revived.

Even before Jesus was nailed to a cross,
By Roman captors, He was treated as dross.
From this alone, many victims would die.
It's beyond words, to fully describe.

The whip used was braided, leather thongs,
Woven in bones of sharp, protruding prongs.
Metal balls added for momentum and weight.
Thirty nine lashes given to their victim of hate.

The whip's sharp bones ripped open His flesh,
His spine exposed was a bloodied mess.
Feeling incredible pain, He went into shock,
In a critical state, before the ordeal of the cross.

Jesus, already faint from extreme blood-loss,
Was laid down and fixed to a crude wooden cross.
Seven inch spikes banged through His wrists and feet.
His grief just begun and mission yet to complete.

His arms stretched out and shoulders dislocate.
Unbearable torment, but what agonies await?
The cross was lifted up, then dropped in a hole.
Caused severe, jarring pain, He couldn't control.

Crucifixion victims died a slow, brutal death.
It was difficult for them to exhale even a breath.
So, Jesus would have to push up with His feet,
To expel another breath, this action repeat.

More pain as His back on the cross did scrape.
From the pressure of nails, there was no escape.
So to exhaustion, He would eventually succumb.
Death was the sure and certain outcome.

Wishing to end pain or hasten one's death,
To make impossible the release of their breath,
The Romans would often break victim's legs.
But when they came to Jesus, He was already dead.

A Roman soldier thrust a spear in His side,
Expelling blood and water, proof He had died.
Roman crucifixion was a harsh way to die.
Masters of their craft, no-one could deny.

There were other things Jesus suffered as well.
Into mental and spiritual anguish He fell.
Deserted by friends and His Heavenly Father.
He endured so much, more than any other.

Knowing my sin is what put Him there,
Is hard to ponder, almost too much to bear.
And to think about how immense was the pain,
He was willing to endure, for my lost soul to gain.

A reasonable person knows that Jesus died.
It's impossible a Roman crucifixion to survive.
Such hurt, what would cause Him to go through?
It could only be immense love for me and for you.

Matt. 27:45–55, Mark 15: 33–41, Luke 23:44–49, John 19:28–37.

DID JESUS RISE?

Jesus died and His body was laid in a tomb.
His followers were mourning, their hearts filled with gloom.
Jesus had said, "In three days I will rise from the dead."
This worried the Jews, not wanting others misled.

They ordered the tomb be sealed 'til the third day,
Lest the disciples come, and take His body away.
At the entrance was placed a large stone and a guard.
If they tried to move it, they would find it very hard.

It was early in the morning, the first day of the week.
Mary Magdalene was at the tomb, His body there to seek.
To anoint Him with spices, her desire and resolve.
To remove the large stone was an issue yet to solve.

Earlier that same morning a violent earthquake,
Terrorised the guards, like dead men, it would make.
There they saw an angel, who rolled the stone away.
To the Chief Priest they reported, what happened on that day.

The Chief Priest met with the elders, a plan was devised.
"Say, while you slept, His disciples their cunning exercised.
They came in the night and took Jesus' body away."
A large reward for this lie, to the soldiers they would pay.

When Mary arrived, she saw the stone rolled away,
From the tomb; on the right, where Jesus' body once lay,
There sat a young man, dressed in a dazzling white robe.
His appearance like lightning, his clothes were white as snow.

He said, "Why do you look for the living among the dead?
He's not here, for He is risen, just exactly like He said."
So she ran to the disciples, this startling news to tell.
Two of them who hurried there, were convinced as well.

Mary stood outside the tomb, while in grief she cried.
She turned, hearing someone ask the reason why?
"I don't know where my Lord is, they've taken Him away."
So she asked this person, "Have you taken Him, I pray?"

She turned to look at Him, though her awareness was dim.
But when Jesus called her "Mary," she realised it was Him.
She went to the disciples and said, "I've seen my Lord."
Because they hadn't seen Him, they doubted Mary's word.

The disciples' doors were locked, the Jewish leaders they feared.
Later that same evening, without warning He appeared.
He said, "Peace be with you." They saw his hands and side,
Were overjoyed that He had risen, it couldn't be denied.

Thomas, one of the twelve, was not with them that night.
He wanted proof He had risen, to see with his own sight.
"Unless I see the hole in His side and the nail marks," he said,
"I will not believe, that Jesus rose from the dead."

Only one week later, they were in the house again.
Thomas was then present, when suddenly Jesus came.
He showed Thomas His hands, and made him feel His side.
"My Lord and my God!" Thomas then to Jesus cried.

On an earlier occasion, two disciples along a road,
Were travelling to Emmaus, with a heavy mental load.
As they talked about the things that had happened at the time,
They were joined by a man, who caught up from behind.

Later sharing a meal, Jesus revealed Himself to them.
Then the same way they'd come, they went back to Jerusalem.
They found the eleven and those assembled there with them.
And told them what occurred, Jesus indeed had risen again.

There were many other people, to whom Jesus did appear.
To over five hundred at once, the Apostle Paul made clear.
So the fact that He rose again is difficult to deny,
With so many first hand witnesses, many still will try.

There's an important observation, we are forced to make.
For fearful men to radically change, what did it really take?
The same ones who left Jesus, at the time of His arrest,
Boldly shared the Gospel, even dying in their quest?

Matthew Ch. 28, Mark Ch. 16, Luke Ch. 24, John Ch. 20, 1 Cor. Ch. 15:6.

GRACE

It's a pleasure, your acquaintance to make.
I am one who enjoys give and take,
In the conversations, we've shared,
And the differing opinions, we've aired.
But it occurs to me, as we're about to part.
Having discussed many matters of the heart.
There's still one thing that causes me pain,
And I fear we may never meet again.

And this often not by our design.
Just circumstances in which we ourselves find.
I realise there may only be one breath,
That separates us from life and death.
As I ponder this and contemplate.
It's true that neither of us knows our fate.
But as we travel and go along our way,
Maybe we each won't see another day.

If I'm concerned for you and really care,
What one thing would I want to share?
What's most important for you to hear?
Of all the thoughts that I hold dear.
Success, power and riches are but three,
Of the goals which people strive to see.
But far more important is for you to be,
Concerned with your eternal destiny.

Your earthy tenure will soon be past.
Only what's done for God will last.   6
And when you see Him face to face,   7
I trust you will know His love and Grace.   8
"Amazing grace how sweet the sound,"
Is a well-known hymn of great renown.
But what is the grace, of which it speaks?
And are there conditions we must meet?

Grace is a free gift, which can't be earned.   9
Through faith received, not to be spurned.
It is freely offered and freely enjoyed.
If we add one thing then grace is destroyed.   10
For grace plus anything, is grace no more.   11
We may think we can work, to add to our score,
That our many works gain God's favour,
But no amount of work can earn our Saviour.

Surely this truth goes against our grain.
It's the reason grace is held in disdain.
But isn't there merit in doing some good?
Doesn't the Bible say that we should?   12
We are saved by grace, through faith alone.   13
In Christ whose perfect life was shown.
For it was only He, who committed no sin,   14
Who could pay the price, our souls to win.

But good works show that our faith is real.
And salvation's soundness they reveal.   15
Deeds follow faith not the other way around.
But in Christ alone, our salvation is found.   16
No matter how good we think we may be,
We're not good enough for salvation to see.
It's only through Christ, the spotless lamb,   17
On our behalf, in God's presence to stand.   18

So, salvation is simple and yet profound.
It's why a stumbling block is often found.   19
We naturally want to work to earn
God's approval, for which we subconsciously yearn
God's Word says plainly, that's not the way.
It is far too simple, some are bound to say.
And there lies the rub, so we will resist.
The good news of salvation, so easily missed.

---

1. Heb. 9:27. 2. 1 Pet. 1:24. 3. Mark 8:36. 4. Eccl. 1:14, 5:10. 5. 2 Cor. 5:10.
6. 1 Cor. 3:13–15. 7. Rom 14:11–12, 2 Cor. 5:10. 8. Eph. 2:8. 9. Eph. 2:8.
10. Eph. 2:9. 11. Rom. 11:6, Gal. 5:1–5. 12. Eph. 2:10. 13. Eph. 2:8. 14. 2 Cor. 5:21.
15. Eph. 2:10, James 2:14–18. 16. 1 Tim. 2:5, Acts 4:12, John 14:6. 17. 1 Pet. 1:19–21.
18. 1 John 2:1. 19. 1 Cor. 1:23.

HE KEEPS TAPPING AT OUR DOOR

Just before Jesus died and rose from the dead,
He met with His disciples and to them He said.
"I am leaving this earth but a comforter I'll send,   1
Your broken saddened hearts He will need to mend.
The promised Holy Spirit to alert men of sin."   2
But He often can't be heard above life's constant din.
We turn our back and wander from Him even more.   3
The gentle Holy Spirit keeps tapping at our door.   4

You behold a sunset its beauty makes you gasp.
Causing a pertinent question of yourself to ask.
"How did this come about, is it nature's random whim,
Or happened just by chance, like the roulette wheel's spin?
Was it carefully designed by a master craftsman's hand?   5
Who could plan and make a masterpiece so grand?"
We push the thought away, rejecting Him once more.   6
The loving Holy Spirit keeps tapping at our door.   7

Sometimes we stand in awe, on a mountain peak.
It's almost as though, we actually hear Him speak.
We reject the very thought and refuse His voice to hear.
A message whispered by the Spirit, into our soul's ear.
Our conscience's calloused edges, now worn very smooth.   8
Can barely hear His voice nor can it our heart move.
But the Spirit is relentless, with His hands now red and raw.
The patient Holy Spirit keeps tapping at our door   9

When we've known financial ruin, in life's normal course
Sickness or a friend's passing, marriage ending in divorce
At such times once again, clearly hearing Him speak,   10
When we weren't even looking, or wanting Him to seek.
And we may have chased after some of life's dreams,
Only to see them shatter. How empty life then seems.
In desperation we've cried out, "There must be more."
The consoling Holy Spirit keeps tapping at our door.   11

If we would open up a bit, and allow Him just one peek,   12
We'd find that He will enter, to our heart He'll speak   13
If we continue to reject Him the Holy Spirit may depart.
Then one day we won't feel Him tugging at our heart.
Our soul's ears won't hear, the eyes of our heart still blind. 14
Many times He tried to speak, but a hardened heart did find.   15
There may come a time, when He'll strive no more.
Sad will be the day when He no longer taps at our door.   16

---

1. John 14:15. 2. John 16:8. 3. Heb. 3:12. 4. Rev. 3:20. 5. Romans 1:20.
6. Heb. 3:15, Rev. 3:20. 7. Rev. 3:20. 8. Eph. 4:18. 9. Rev. 3:20. 10. Matt. 11:28–30.
11. Rev. 3:20. 12. Prov. 3:5. 13. Rev. 3:20. 14. Matt 13:10–15. 15. Heb. 3:7–12.
16. Heb. 6:4–6.

I NEVER KNEW YOU
HAUNTING WORDS

Is any 'lostness' worse than being lost, thinking you're found?
Believing you firmly stand, while standing on shaky ground.   1
But many will travel that road that Jesus called the Broad Way.   2
Are any so wretched, as some who go to church and even pray?
Like a man who sips desert sand, thinking water is in his cup,   3
How tragic for him who thinks, all the good he's done adds up.   4
For he may have done mighty works for the Lord along the way.
Of all those who Jesus knows, "I never knew you," He will say.   5

Plunging into the afterlife without thought is one form of grief.
But playing a saint and being deceived, thinking you have belief,
Is Satan's fraud, for all those who call on the Name of the Lord,   6
Believing that to say the words that were written in His Word,
Would guarantee a place in Heaven, without a change of life.   7
To hear those words writ large, will cut the soul just like a knife.
For when they meet God face to face, on that Judgement Day.   8
Of all those who Jesus knows, "I never knew you," He will say.

Like Bible readers and church attenders, around in Jesus' day,   9
You can become lost in a dream, convinced you know the way.
Meanwhile you are travelling to hell and, in church clothes.   10
The ones who are truly His, the Shepherd of the sheep knows.   11
Oblivious you continue on your familiar and well-worn path,
Blind to the reckoning that will happen in the aftermath.   12
No matter that you call Him Lord, your affection for Him convey,
Of all those who Jesus knows, "I never knew you," He will say.

"Lord, didn't we prophesy and cast out demons in your Name?"   13
But hearers and not doers of the Word, put God to shame.   14
"Not all who call me Lord, Lord, will enter Heaven's doorway.
But only those who do My Father's will," did Jesus say.
But Jesus' words are before us, glowing as if engraved by fire.
We have the right doctrine, while sinking deeper into the mire.
Mere head knowledge of God's Word, will not our sins allay.
Of all those who Jesus knows, "I never knew you," He will say.

It is true that we are saved by grace and through faith alone.   15
But faith itself is not alone, by our righteous works is shown.   16
Abraham was called, he knew not where, but by faith obeyed.
And his wife Sarah gave birth to a son when to God He prayed.   17
If faith is real we grow in holiness and more like Christ to be,   18
And put to death deeds of the flesh, the Holy Spirit in us sees.   19
Ever hearing the Spirit's voice, but His warnings don't obey.   20
Of all those who Jesus knows, "I never knew you," He will say.

At times we feel and act like saints, our lives still marked by sin.
Because we fail to allow God's Word to change us from within.   21
We carry hatred for a brother and others we refuse to forgive.
And often hear God's Word, but it changes not how we live.   22
But if our righteousness does not exceed the Pharisees',   23
Secure in God we may feel, but Him we will not please.
To hear those shocking words, will leave us standing in dismay.
Of all those who Jesus knows, "I never knew you," He will say.

---

1. Matt. 7:26–27. 2. Luke 13:23–30. 3. Isaiah 29:8. 4. Eph. 2:9. 5. Matt. 7: 21–23.
6. Rom. 10:13. 7. James 1:23–25. 8. 2 Cor. 5:10. 9. Matt. 23:27. 10. Matt. 25:41.
11. John 10:27. 12. 2 Cor. 5:10. 13. Matt. 7:22. 14. Matt. 7:21–27, Luke 6:46.
15. Eph. 2:8. 16. Heb. 11:8–19. 17. Gen. 15:2–6. 18. Heb. 12:14, 1 Peter 1:15–16.
19. Rom. 8:13. 20. Heb. 3:15. 21. James 1:21–22. 22. Matt. 7:26-27, 2 Tim. 3:16–17.
23. Matt. 5:20.

LIVING ON THE SCRATCH

Imagine you're standing in a room, a wire in front of you.
Left and right in both directions, stretched very tightly too.
You take a sharp instrument, lean forward and make a mark.
An illustration we now share, on life's message we embark.

The wire represents eternity, in both ways forever goes.
The scratch just like your life, on a point of time it froze.
Whether your life lasts many, or only a few more years.　　1
You will soon be forgotten, once earthly life disappears.　　2

Some believe life ends at death, we may believe it, or not.　　3
We know that at the end of it, others get the things we've got.　　4
And the length of life on earth, is not the most important thing.
It may be short but well lived, when we each face death's sting.

What matters is a quality life … leaving a strong legacy;
All-important leave-behinds, abstract things we cannot see.
Like the way we care for others and help improve their lives.　　5
Unlike the things we touch, on which the whole world thrives.　　6

We place a lot of value on the many things we own.　　7
Of far greater worth is the love, that in others' lives we've sown.　　8
Those qualities and values live through all eternity,
By those who follow the example, they, in our lives, did see.　　9

When we know God it matters little, if life is long or short.
It's better to live it gracefully, to do the things we ought.　　10
And we know these things may often take a whole life-time to learn.
Salvation freely given by grace, we offer others in return.　　11

The Spirit doesn't force us, He wants us to co-operate.
For in a fully yielded heart the gentle Spirit will operate.   12
Faults can be like dust, which lightly dusted don't remain.
Some need a harder scrub for they leave a deeper stain.   13

Good works are produced by faith, but don't salvation earn.   14
If we can simply trust in Him, to live by His grace we learn.
Nothing better can we do for those who are watching what we do,
Than to help them come to God, and find their loving Saviour too.   15

Then there's no need to cling to life, or to fear eternity.   16
We'll stand before God in His time, not simply cease to be.   17
Everyone will face a reckoning of life lived poorly or well.   18
Even if we think we won't, or don't believe in Hell.   19

God's Word talks about a place that we would hesitate to see.
If He left us in this world, in a type of Hell we'd already be.
No matter how we picture Hell, it's not a place we'd like to know.
We'd much rather be in Heaven, and with our loving Saviour go.

---

1. 1 Tim. 6:13, 1 Pet. 1:24. 2. Eccl. 9:5. 3. Heb. 9:27. 4. Luke 12:20. 5. Phil. 2:4.
6. Col. 3:2. 7. Matt. 6: 19-21. 8. Gal. 6:10. 9. Matt. 5:16. 10. 1 John 1:7. 11. 2 Tim. 2:1-2.
12. Rom. 8:1-4. 13. Ps. 51:1-2, John 16:8, 1 John 1:9. 14. Eph. 2:8-9. 15. Mark 16:15-16.
16. James 4:14. 17. Heb. 9:27. 18. Matt. 25:31-40, 2 Cor. 5:10. 19. Rev. 21:8.

OUR GOD IS IN CONTROL

As we live our life's journey, exploring many roads,
We oft' times discover, we must carry heavy loads.
And though at times we find the weight is hard to bear.   1
Jesus tells us in His Word, He was before us there.   2
To cast our cares upon Him, and us He will console.   3
We can rest in our all-loving God, for He is in control.   4

He doesn't promise us we'll be free of earthly pain.
But says He'll be with us, having suffered the same.   5
Afflictions may startle us, but they're no surprise to Him.   6
He knows in advance they will come, our disposition grim.   7
He's always there to lift our gloomy, despondent soul,   8
As we rest in our all-present God, for He is in control.   9

At times we may be overcome by a spirit of deep fear.   10
We focus on our circumstance, forgetting He is near.   11
If we would raise our drooping eyes to a higher gaze,
Stormy seas around us, our spirits no longer faze.   12
Fix our thoughts on Christ, make Him our primary goal,   13
And rest upon our all-powerful God, for He is in control.   14

If we were without our Lord, how would we ever cope?
Many do not know Him, they don't enjoy our living hope   15
It's not as though we need our hope to use it as a crutch,
It is the confidence to know, we are safely in His clutch.   16
So, despite the seas around us, His name we will extol,   17
And rest in our all-knowing God, for He is in control.   18

---

1. John 16:33. **2.** 1 Pet. 2:21. **3.** 1 Pet. 5:7. **4.** 1 John 4:7–8 **5.** Isaiah 43:2, 1 Pet. 5:9–10.
6. Rom. 8:16–17. **7.** Matt. 6:8, Phil. 1:29. **8.** James 4:9-10. **9.** Ps. 139:7–12. **10.** 2 Tim 1:7.
11. Matt. 14:29–30. **12.** Mark 4:37–39. **13.** Heb. 3:1. **14.** Ps. 147:5, Jer. 32:17.
15. Rom. 5:3-5. **16.** Matt. 23:37, John 10:28-29. **17.** Ps. 145:1–2. **18.** Ps. 147:5.

REGRET TURNS TO JOY

The old man rocks himself gently, in his comfy chair.
If only he could talk with mates, but none of them are there.
They have all left God's waiting room and into eternity passed.
Never in his wildest dreams, did he think he would be last.
So often lost in his thoughts, he'd see out most of his days.
And to help him pass the time, he would even sometimes pray.
He used to be so active, but those days were now long gone.
Thinking back he was amazed, at where his energy came from.

Time moves now so slowly, that he often will just doze.
For over ninety years he's lived, forgotten more than he knows.
He's rather proud of his life, all things considered, a great success.
The many things that he owns, the proof they do attest.
He has a good reputation, a better leader you couldn't find.
He could have been anything, to which he applied his mind.
And being philanthropic, as all his friends did know,
He would always do the right thing, even to church would go.

He lived a full and prosperous life, still there was some regret.
So many actions of the flesh, he'd rather just forget.
Hoping God will not remember them, or hold him to account.
If God did, what could he say, or what defence could mount?
Thinking on past years he says, "What more could I have done,
To make God more pleased with me, and His favour to have won?
I could have read the Bible more, but didn't have spare time.
But I did believe its message and He knows this heart of mine."

Yes, God doesn't on the outside look, but sees a person's heart. 2

He knows who are really His, from His clutch they won't depart 3

What we do is well and good ... a part of worship too. 4

But if we think by merit we deserve Heaven by what we do, 5

We'll be very disappointed, when we before Him stand.

Our lives may be a great success, but not what He had planned. 6

For it's not the things we do in life, but it is what Christ has done.

He took the punishment for our sins. God gave His only Son. 7

So, what is it God wants from us? What is it we must do?

To honour Him, His precepts keep, is the duty of me and you. 8

And to love Him with all our heart, soul, mind and strength. 9

Telling others of His wondrous love, we should go to any length. 10

Meditating upon Jesus in our lives, bringing glory to our Lord. 11

Listening to His Holy Spirit as He teaches us His Word. 12

Growing to be like Jesus, to love Him more, His plans fulfil. 13

Many who cry out "Lord," only enter Heaven if they do His will. 14

The old man thinks about all of this and what he must put right.

Gradually, into his weak old heart, the Holy Spirit shines a light. 15

He struggles off his comfy chair, stoops on wobbly, bended knees,

And says a prayer from His heart, with His Saviour he pleads. 16

He confesses he's lived his life, upon his own selfish terms,

And invites Jesus into his heart, which the Holy Spirit confirms. 17

He knows at once, he's now the Lord's, for all eternity ... 18

Then he takes his final breath and goes home with his Lord to be. 19

---

1. Eph. 2:8–9. 2. 1 Sam. 16:7, Jer. 17:10. 3. John 10:27–28. 4. Prov. 21:3, Jer. 7:21–23. 5. Eph. 2:8–10. 6. Jer. 29:11. 7. 1 Pet. 2:24. 8. Eccl. 12:13. 9. Matt. 22:37. 10. Matt. 28:19–20, 1 Cor. 9:16. 11. Ps. 63:6, 104:34. 12. John 14:26. 13. Rom 12:2, Phil. 2:5–8, 3:10. 14. Matt. 7:21. 15. John 16:8. 16. 1 John 1:9. 17. Eph. 1:13. 18. John 10:27–28, Rom. 8:16. 19. 2 Cor. 5:8.

SIN NO MORE – APOSTLE JOHN

The One whom we saw, heard and touched,
Who gave us His all and loved us so much.
From God the Father, the Word of Life came,
And Eternal Life to us, He would proclaim.

We testify about Christ Jesus the Word,
Whom we have handled and we have heard.
And this is the reason for which He came.
To offer us salvation in His Holy name.

His message is that God is the Light.
There's no darkness in Him, as of the night.
But if in darkness we continue to walk,
To claim to know Him, is just talk.

We are liars and the truth do not know.
As the falsehoods from our mouth do show.
If we claim no sin, we ourselves deceive,
Yet say in Him, we trust and believe.

But we are making Him out to be a liar.
And bogging our souls in a spiritual mire,
If we say we have fellowship with Him,
But keep on wilfully walking in sin.

I speak of habitual sin of course.
That is wilful sin, with no remorse.
I write that you would sin no more,
But sin is ever crouching at the door.

So if we then, our sins confess.
We're covered by His righteousness.
Because He is faithful and will forgive,
He will cleanse us, so in Him we can live.

So if we are walking in God's light,
We can with His help, live our lives aright.
There are still times when we may fail,
Of Jesus' righteousness we then avail. 3

Then for sin, what's to be our attitude?
The price is paid, He has our gratitude.
But it's still not fine to choose to sin.
This shows an unchanged heart within. 4

I would that you, not continue in sin,
But the battle over your flesh to win. 5
And if you find that sin you do.
An Advocate stands there waiting for you. 6

Christ Jesus has risen from the dead.
By God's throne there in your stead, 7
He presents the Father with your case,
And you're always covered by His grace.

---

1 John Chs. 1 and 2. 1. Acts 4:12. 2. Gen. 4:7. 3. 2 Cor. 5:21, 1 Pet. 2:24, Rom. 4:5.
4. Acts 8:21–22, Rom. 8:7, Eph. 2:3. 5. Rom 8: 23–24. 6. 1 John 2:1. 7. Rom 8:34.

STUFF

We tread a long, endless path, in our pursuit of stuff.   1
If it becomes obsessive, then we'll never have enough.   2
You need not be religious for this truth to see.
Many who are worldly wise, make this discovery.

We can all be guilty of wanting a new, shiny toy.   3
And so that we can own it, many excuses we employ.
We're convinced that we need it, when it's really a *want*.
We may provoke some envy, before others we can flaunt.

We might think we deserve it, and entertain the thought,
"It's a reward for our efforts, for the toil we have wrought."
But no sooner do we have it, or achieve that cherished thing,
Than we move to our next goal, our energies to fling.

When it really comes down to it, what basics do we need?
It is shelter, clothing and food, upon which we daily feed.
The Word of God has much to say about this matter too.
"Seek first the Kingdom, these things will be added unto you."   4

Jesus did not promise we'll have a life of luxury.
He said that He would supply everything we need.   5
And "Look at the birds of the air, who do not sow or reap,   6
Or store food in barns, yet our Father them does keep.

And see the lilies of the field, they don't labour or spin,
Dressed better than Solomon, more magnificent than him.
Don't worry about what you'll eat, drink or even wear,
Your Heavenly Father knows, of your needs is fully aware."

It's not so wrong to have these things, but what's the priority?
When God blesses us, a blessing to others we can be.
This challenge is for each of us, for how much is enough?
We may have sufficient, while others do it tough.

You say that you're not wealthy, with others you compare,
Yet if you visit Africa, you're an instant millionaire.
And it puts things in perspective, when a crisis I see.
I should use things to serve people, not use people to serve me.

Some say that it is God's reward, when He gives them things.
Proof of faith's not measured thus, so an alarm bell rings!
In our attempt to justify the possessions that we chase,
We may neglect those needing help, and from our minds erase.

Do we believe the more we have, the more we can disburse?
Seeing wealth as blessing, but perhaps a deceptive curse?
We may be snared in a trap, a delusion, a fine line.
The more I have to give away, the more I keep that's mine.   7

But money's not the problem, the love of it is worse.   8
We may say that we love our God, but do we put Him first?   9
If we want to follow Christ, promised suffering we will see.   10
"Where your treasure is," He said, "that's where your heart will be."   11

You cannot serve two masters, you'll hate one and love the other.   12
You can't serve God and money or ignore the needs of a brother."   13
How to settle this dilemma, how to get the balance right?
If we give all we have away, we'll rely on others in our plight.

It's clear that we should work, so to not depend on others.   14
God supplies our needs, so we can share things with our brothers.   15
We can help those who God puts directly in our way   16
Looking for His guidance, as we walk with Him each day.

Remembering always Jesus' Words and in our lives employ,
"Don't save earthly treasure, where moth and rust destroy."   17
Set our minds on things above, not things upon the earth.   18
And to be content and happy, is really of great worth.   19

For if a man gains the whole world but loses His own soul.
What profit would that be to Him, to pay this heavy toll?   20
Many things over a lifetime, mankind collects and stores.   21
Only what leaves earth with you, can you say is really yours.   22

---

1. 1 John 2:16. **2.** Eccl. 5:10. **3.** 1 John 2:16. **4.** Matt 6:33. **5.** Phil. 4: 19. **6.** Matt 6:26–34.
7. 1 Tim 6:9–10. **8.** 1 Tim 6:10. **9.** Mark 12:30–31. **10.** Luke 9:23, Phil 1:29, 2 Tim. 2:3.
11. Matt 6:21 **12.** Matt 6:24. **13.** James 2:15-16. **14.** Eph. 4:28. **15.** Heb. 13:16, Prov. 22:9.
16. Luke 16:19-31. **17.** Matt 6:19–21. **18.** Col. 3:2. **19.** Heb. 13:5, 1 Tim. 6:6–8.
20. Matt 16:26. **21.** Luke 12:15. **22.** 2 Cor. 4:18.

THE ARMOUR OF GOD

The day of our salvation, we gladly celebrate. 1
To live new lives afresh, we can hardly wait.
Being wholly born again and a new creation made, 2
As the Holy Spirit helps us, we see our old lives fade. 3

But the Word of God warns us, we have an adversary. 4
Not against flesh and blood will our only struggles be.
We'll fight dark, spiritual forces, rulers and authorities.
Powers in heavenly realms, all part of Satan's strategies.

We stand strong in the Lord and in His mighty power.
Put on God's full armour to fight Satan every hour.
So when the day of evil comes, we can stand our ground.
When the Evil One attacks, in God's strength we're found.

Standing with the Belt of Truth, firmly around our waist,
The Breastplate of Righteousness in its proper place,
Our feet shod with readiness, from the Gospel of Peace,
And with the Sword of the Spirit, secure in its sheath.

Faith's shield protects us, when the devil's arrows flame.
And the Helmet of Salvation, as the Word of God we claim.
Abiding in the Spirit, with many requests and prayer.
Always being alert, praying for people in His care.

This truth may seem straight forward, but what does it really mean?
How do we apply it against an enemy unseen?
It's of utmost importance and a Christian needs to know.
The Word says if we resist him, Satan has to go. 5

With the Belt of Truth around our waist, upon it we rely.
We should only say what's true, not be caught out in a lie.
One who walks in truth, will in all his ways be free.
Untruths allow Satan entry, while truth makes him flee.

Alternative truths cannot exist, each of them can't be right.
So when Jesus said, "I am the way, the truth and the life,"
One path to Heaven He made plain, on this we cannot sway.
If we firmly stand on gospel truth, Satan must give way.

The Breastplate of Righteousness, will our hearts protect.
We can't defeat dark powers, with our own righteousness.
If we're clothed in Christ, in His righteousness be found,
The devil is defeated, for we stand on solid ground.

Our feet need protection too, as we battle evil powers.
Or they won't stand harsh rigour, of fighting many hours.
So, hard places we traverse with protection on our feet,
Hardship unapparent, shod with the Gospel of Peace.

The Shield of Faith against Satan's arrows will also protect,
When positioned in an arrow's path, its deadly aim deflect.
With false thoughts, feelings, fear and lies, a foothold he secures.
Our faith's firm foundation protects against the devil's lures.

The Helmet of Salvation guards from attacks upon the mind.
If we're secure in salvation's hope, it's then that we will find,
A shield against discouragement, Satan's conquest allayed,
Assurance of our salvation firm, the weapons of evil stayed.

With the Sword of the Spirit, against evil we strike back.
We turn from defending and upon spiritual powers attack.
But we cannot use this sword, unless His Word we know.
With the living Word rightly applied, the enemy must go.

Ephesians Ch. 6:10–18. 1. Luke 15:7. 2. 2 Cor. 5:17. 3. John 14:15–18. 4. 1 Peter 5:8.
5. James 4:7.

THE DEITY OF CHRIST

In the beginning God created the heavens and the earth.   1
He looked upon His creation, with warm feelings of mirth.   2
And God's Spirit hovered over the waters of the deep.   3
All things by His powerful Word, God does hold and keep.   4

In the beginning was the Word and the Word was God.   5
Was with God from the very start, yet on this earth He trod.   6
The Word became flesh and made His dwelling among men.   7
Provided purification for sin and returned to God's side again.   8

In these last days God has spoken to us through His Son.   9
Made Him heir of all things, mighty works He has done.
He's the radiance of God's glory, the writer of Hebrews said.
Exact representation of His being, so do not be misled.

Listen to the words, God about Him did proclaim,
"Your throne, O God, will enjoy an everlasting reign.   10
In the beginning, Lord, you laid the foundations of the earth.   11
The very heavens were created by Your Hands at work."

John said, "No-one's ever seen God, but God the only One.   12
He who is sitting at the Father's side, is His only Son.   13
And without Him was nothing made, that has indeed been made."   14
The Father and Son are both God, this truth we can't evade.   15

---

1. Gen. 1:1. **2.** Gen. 1:31. **3.** Gen. 1:2. **4.** Heb. 1:3, Col. 1:17. **5.** John 1:1–2. **6.** John 1:2. **7.** John 1:14. **8.** Heb. 1:3. **9.** Heb. 1:1–3. **10.** Heb. 1:8. **11.** Heb. 1:10. **12.** John 1:18. **13.** John 1:18, Heb. 1:3. **14.** John 1:3. **15.** 1 Cor. 8:6.

THE FATHER'S HEART

Jesus, long ago to a crowd this story told.
A Father had two sons who were under his control.
He had a wayward son and a faithful elder brother.
They were very different, compared to one another.

The young one anxious, he could no longer wait.
He entreated his father for a share of his estate.
The Father, his estate, between them did divide.
The younger son left, not with them now to reside.

So he spent all his money on very wild living.
His wealth to prostitutes, he was now giving.
And after some time his money was all gone.
When severe famine came, food he then had none.

He became impoverished, in ever greater need.
For a job with a pig farmer, he was glad to plead.
And even the pods that he watched the pigs eat,
Could fill his stomach and his despair would meet.

But no-one who was there would give him anything.
Even though He starved, food they would not bring.
He thought about His family, if he were only there.
There would be food aplenty and even some to spare.

So, after a while when to his senses finally he came.
He knew that he could only have himself to blame.
He said, "I'll return home and this is what I'll say,
'I am sorry for leaving you and going far away.

I've sinned against Heaven and sinned against you.
I'm not a worthy son and I know that this is true.
So please can you make me just like your hired men?'"
So he straightway got up, and then went home again.

He travelled very far and his trip was not quite done.
When, full of compassion, the father ran to his son,
Threw his arms around him and kissed him with glee.
He had yearned so much for his lost son to see.

Ordering his servants, "Quick, my son we must treat.
Fetch him a ring, my best robe and sandals for his feet,
And bring the fattened calf and then with the beast,
We will celebrate and have a wonderful feast."

The older brother was angry so refused to go in.
His father went out and then did plead with him.
His son said, "For all these years I slaved for you.
There's nothing you've asked for that I wouldn't do.

You gave me no goat to celebrate with my friends.
He spent all his money, yet him you do defend.
For your wayward son who squandered all his wealth,
You killed a fattened calf for others and yourself."

The father said, "Son, you've faithfully done your chores.
You've always been with me and all I have is yours.
But your brother who was lost, has now been found.
He has come home again and is safe and sound."

It's not too difficult, the lesson for all to see.
The father pictures God, the lost son, you and me.
Every one of us like sheep have gone astray.   1
Each one of us has turned, gone our own way.

Our Heavenly Father with His outstretched arms,
Longs to hold us close, within His loving palms.
So everyone in His clutch can never be removed,   2
Eternally there by love, He has so often proved.

As any loving parent is aware and does surely know.
The length for our children, we're prepared to go.
When they struggle with trials and stresses of this life,
With arms wide open we're there, to rescue them from strife.

Luke Ch.15. 1. Isaiah 53:6. 2. John 10:28.

THE GOD MAN

Some say while on earth Jesus was a mere man.
He laid aside His divinity as part of God's plan.
So let me ask you how it could possibly be,
That He was only human, just like you and me?　　　　1

His mother was Mary and His Father was divine.
God sent forth His Son in the fullness of time.　　　　2
Born of a woman, so His humanity is defined.
And from God's Spirit, His Fatherhood assigned.

But what were the claims that Jesus did make,
When the Jews accused Him of being a fake?
They picked up rocks, intending Him to stone,　　　　3
After He told them, "I and the Father are one."

He asked, "For which of these miracles I've shown,
Do you want to kill me, by having me stoned?"
"For none of these wonders," was their reply.
"But a man claiming to be God should die."

There were other claims which Jesus did make.
To forgive men their sins and their penalty to take.　　　　4
But only God can forgive sins, of that we are sure
The Pharisees knew it was written in the Law.　　　　5

The Pharisees tried to set the record straight.
But Jesus their traps would always anticipate.
He said "Punishment one day, you will receive.　　　　6
Because, God has come and you don't believe".

"He who's seen me, the Father has seen."	7
Surely more claims to be God, it would seem.
He even said "Before Abraham, I did exist."	8
Yet another claim to His Deity, He did insist.

It pleased God in Him, to have His fullness dwell.
All things to Him reconciled by the cross as well.	9
Jesus said, "All that belongs to the Father is mine."	10
So could He make that claim if He wasn't divine?

And of deceptive ideas the Apostle Paul did tell.	11
The human traditions on which men like to dwell.
He said, "In Christ lives the fullness of the Deity.
He's God in bodily form, whom we all can see."

And so it's hard to say Jesus was only a man.
When His words are examined, they do firmly stand.
And would we dare say that our Lord was mistaken.
When His claims in God's Word, together are taken?

We are saved, only by faith in Christ alone.	12
He led a sinless life and for our sins did atone.	13
If in Jesus, an ordinary man, only, was found.
Faith's very foundations would then run aground.

---

1. Phil. Ch. 2. 2. Gal. 4:4. 3. John 10:33. 4. Heb. 8:12, Mark 2:5–7. 5. Jer. 31:34.
6. Luke 19:44. 7. John 14:9. 8. John 8:58. 9. Col. 1:19. 10. John 16:15. 11. Col. 2:8–9.
12. 1 Tim. 2:5, Acts 4:12, John 14:6. 13. 2 Cor. 5:21.

THE GOOD SAMARITAN

Jesus was confronted by an expert in the law,
Testing Him to see just what conclusion He would draw.
He asked, "What must I do to gain eternal life?"
He tried to expose Jesus, so causing Him some strife.
Jesus answered, "How do you then read the Law?
How do you understand it and a conclusion draw?"
He then asked the man the scriptures, him to quote.
The lawyer, well versed in them, confidently spoke:

"Love the Lord your God, with all your heart,
Your soul, strength and mind," but this is only part.
The scripture also says it's important what we do,
'Love our neighbour as our self.' We must do this too.
Jesus then commended him, for he answered very well,
And instructed him to go and live the way the scriptures tell.
"You are right," Jesus said. "Do this and you will live."
Then to pose another question … a problem, to Jesus give:

"Who then is my neighbour, can you now explain?"
He cited two commandments. To keep them could he claim?
Jesus said, "A man who went from Jerusalem to Jericho,
Was set upon by robbers who stripped him of his clothes.
They beat him and then left, the poor man was half dead.
But people passed him by, as from his wounds he bled.
The first was a priest, who passed on the other side.
Then a Levite saw him too, and equal caution he applied.

An enemy of the Jews, a Samaritan came along,   2
He dressed the poor man's wounds to make him very strong.
He put him on his donkey and took him to an inn.
Gave money to the manager, to look after him.
Said he would return and pay other expenses that he had.
To restore him back to health, he would be very glad.
"Who was the true neighbour, of the man so nearly dead?"
"The one who showed him mercy," the expert lawyer said.

So then Jesus told the lawyer that this he too must do.
"Love your God with all your heart, and love your neighbour too."
The story gives us insight to the neighbour *we* should see.
They may well be unlike us … will be anyone in need.
But was there another subtlety in the question that he posed?
Not only who our neighbour is, but who isn't, I propose.
For him to ask Jesus for "our neighbour" to define,
Was it just an excuse for others' needs to decline?

Can we draw such conclusions and credibility not exceed?
Are there other obvious lessons in this story that we read?
Was the victim very foolish to decide to travel there?
Robbers were so common then, he should have been aware.
We often put our neighbours into separate categories;
One deserving of our help, another our help never sees.
The Samaritan is a picture of Christ who sees the poor.
Their plight He can't walk past, their wounds He can't ignore.

What excuses do we have, to pass on the other side?
We often do the same, our confession we cannot hide.
So we must follow Christ, with compassion He was moved.
Rescues us from our wounds, but He, Himself was so abused.
This doesn't come just naturally, our selfishness we confess,
For us to truly love others, we His Spirit must possess.
If we keep the entire law, but of one point guilty be,
We have broken all of it, His mercy, our only plea.   3

Luke 10:25–37. 1. Gal. 5:14. 2. Isaiah 53:3. 3. James 2:10.

THE HOLY SPIRIT

Jesus met with His disciples, soon to play His part,
Of dying on a cross and then for Heaven depart.
As they gathered around Him, He spoke to them from His heart.
And gave them instructions, for their ministry to start.

He said, "I'm going to the Father, once this earth I leave,
But wait until the promised Holy Spirit you receive.
In Jerusalem this will happen, so please do tarry there.
He will come and fill you, with His power to share.

The Father will send the one the world cannot accept.
He'll be another counsellor and Him they will reject.
Neither will they know Him and Him they will not see.
You know Him, He lives with you, and in you He will be.

Soon the world will not see, but you'll again see Me.
I will not leave you alone, orphans you shall not be.
The Holy Spirit Whom the Father will send in my Name,
Will teach you all things and in my ways He'll train.

He will also remind you of everything I have said.
This will happen once I have risen from the dead.
Peace I leave with you, My peace now give to you.
Do not let your hearts be troubled, for the Spirit is true.

And do not be afraid, because I will be coming back.
The Spirit of Truth will ensure that you nothing lack.
He goes out from the Father and will testify of Me.
Unless I go away, the Father won't send Him to thee.

But when I go away, I can send Him to you.
Convicting the world of guilt, is one thing He will do.
In regard to sin because men don't believe in Me,
He will guide in all truth, so that men can finally see.

He will not speak on His own, but only what He hears.
Give you supernatural strength and calm all your fears,
He will tell you what to expect, what is yet to come.
So you will know in advance, that the battle's won.

Everything the Spirit does, brings glory back to Me.
He takes of what is mine and causes you then to see.
All that belongs to the Father also belongs to Me.
That's why He takes of mine and makes it known to thee."

We've only scratched the surface, His Word does us inform.
There are many other functions, the Spirit does perform.
He regenerates our hearts, empowers us and guides.
He intercedes on our behalf and purifies inside.

He comes into our hearts, with refining fire and power,
To remove the grit and grime, our inner lives to scour.
Secret thoughts, hidden sin, a light on them does shine.
When with them He has dealt, He further will refine.

On hearing the Word of Truth, we are included in Christ.
Believing the gospel of salvation, by the Holy Spirit enticed.
We are marked in Him, with the promised Spirit's seal,
As a deposit guaranteeing, God's ownership made real.

John Chs. 14–16. Eph. Ch. 2, Rom Ch. 8:26.

THE KINGDOM OF HEAVEN

By "the Kingdom of Heaven," what did Jesus mean?
He told stories and parables, the truth for us to glean.
And unless, as little children, we are willing to become,   1
We can never enter there, our place cannot be won.
By becoming just like children, what do we understand?
How do we secure a place, or stay on sinking sand?   2
A child comes to its father in faith and humility.
We must likewise come to God if salvation wish to see.

It takes a broken person to humbly confess their pride.   3
To own up to their sin and rebellion that's inside.   4
That's how the Kingdom's entered for here now is the thing;
Surrendering to His Lordship we proclaim that Christ is King.   5
For the Kingdom of our God is where He reigns supreme.   6
It can be within our hearts and around us also seen.   7
Our lives, an extension of His Kingdom here on the earth,
If we become a new creation, experiencing new birth.   8

To show the Kingdom's value, Jesus a story told,
Of a man who found a special pearl, as precious as pure gold.   9
Sold everything he owned to have that rare gemstone.
The Kingdom is worth far more than anything we own.
He told the story of a man, who planted a mustard seed.   10
The smallest of all the seeds, yet became a massive tree.
And within its branches, the birds all came to nest.
His Kingdom is now worldwide and within it we can rest.

Then a story of ten virgins, outside a wedding feast,   11
Waiting for the bridegroom while their worries did increase.
Five of them were foolish and five of them were wise.
The foolish ones were unprepared, which led to their demise.
The wise ones trimmed their lamps, and carried extra oil.
The others' oil soon ran out, their hearts now in turmoil.
When they went to buy some more, a dilemma then arose.
The bridegroom arrived soon after and the door was tightly closed.

Returning they cried out, "Lord will you open up the door?
It's not our fault we had no oil, and needed to get more."
"I know you not," He then replied, "You were far too slow.
The day, or the hour I come, you will never know."
A man who gave a dinner party and invited many guests,   12
Hearing his friends' excuses, put his patience to the test.
In anger he called his servants to go out into the streets,
Tell the poor, blind and crippled to come enjoy the feast.

After they had done this, they found there was still room.
They invited those on roads and lanes and discovered very soon,
The master's house was very full and all were fully fed.
"None of those invited, will taste my banquet," the man said.
Other stories Jesus told, but the message was quite clear;
Those who do not enter are the ones who need to fear.
He'll return unexpectedly, in the twinkling of an eye.
When this present age ends, or we'll meet him when we die.

---

1. Matt. 18:3. 2. Matt 7:26. 3. Prov. 18:12. 4. Heb. 3:15. 5. 1 Tim.1:16–17, Rev. 11:15.
6. Daniel 7:14. 7. Luke 17:21, Col. 1:12-14. 8. John 3:3, 2 Cor. 5:17. 9. Matt 13: 45–46.
10. Matt 13:31–32. 11. Matt 25:1–13. 12. Luke 14:15–24.

THE ONE WHO SAT AT JESUS' FEET

When a Pharisee asked Him to dine,
At Simon's table Jesus did incline.
It was Him whom Simon wished to meet,
He prepared a meal for them to eat.
But an unwelcome guest soon arrived,
And when she made her way inside,
She began to loudly wail and to weep.
She was the one who sat at Jesus' feet.

It seems she was a lady of the night,
Desperate for some hope and light.
Despite her critics and her great fears,
She stooped in brokenness and tears.
But where was this lowly woman from?
And even though she had done wrong,
And the many laws she'd failed to keep,
She was the one who sat at Jesus' feet.

With her tears she made them wet.
But she had hardly finished yet.
Ignoring Simon's disapproving stare,
Wiped then clean with her long hair.
Expensive perfume she then did pour,
Then lavishly she added some more.
Not concerned with being discreet.
She was the one who sat at Jesus' feet.

"Are you really a prophet?" Simon thought.
"Have you not been correctly taught?
This kind of woman, you should know,
Who's touching you, she needs to go."
So, Simon who was very quick to judge,
With his criticisms was hard to budge.
This humble woman could not defeat.
She was the one who sat at Jesus' feet

Knowing his thoughts Jesus undeterred,
To make clear where he knew he erred,
Told Simon a tale of two indebted men,
With differing amounts owed by them.
Jesus wanted to open Simon's mind.
So, he also truth would be able to find.
This woman he would be glad to meet.
She was the one who sat at Jesus' feet.

Simon steadfastly observed the law.
For God, could he have done more?
But Jesus loved the Pharisee as well,
And so, the story he continued to tell.
He saw the inner reaches of his heart,
Which must break before He departs.
Simon must repent of prideful conceit,
And observe the one who sat at Jesus' feet

"So, one man owed little, the other a great deal,"
Then Jesus asked Simon, "Which one do you feel,
If the total debts were cancelled for them both,
Which one of the men would love the lender most?"
He said, "I suppose the one with the biggest debt."
Then Jesus answered, "Simon, you are correct."
He looked lovingly upon the woman meek.
She was the one who sat at Jesus' feet.

"Simon, you loved little, she loved me more.
You didn't warmly greet me at your door.
No water, or kiss, or oil to anoint my head,
But this dear woman did all that instead."
Turning to her He said, "Your sin I forgive.
You will now find out how to truly live.
Your faith has saved you so go in peace."
She was the one who sat at Jesus' feet.

Luke 7:36–50.

THE PROPHET DANIEL

Nebuchadnezzar was King of Babylon, around 605 BC,
He besieged Jerusalem, taking the Jews into captivity.
The Lord allowed this punishment for a time of seventy years,
Because they worshipped idols and God they did not fear.

The King ordered his chief official into his service to bring,
Men of Israel's royalty who would come to serve the King.
Young, smart men with no defect and qualified to serve,
To learn the local language, special food for them reserved.

The official selected several men and with them Daniel chose,
Who didn't follow the King's diet and to him did not disclose.
Daniel and three friends ate vegetables, with water only to drink.
They looked better than all the others, and even better could they think.

God gave them knowledge, learning and understanding minds.
Daniel could interpret dreams and visions of many kinds.
When the King spoke on many matters with Daniel and his friends,
Their advice was ten times better, than all the other men.

In the second year of his reign, the King dreamt and couldn't sleep.
Into his troubled mind, anxiety and stress began to creep.
He called for his advisers to interpret what he'd seen,
To tell him what his dream was, as well as what it means.

They said that no-one on this earth could tell him such a thing.
That such a difficult task had never been asked by any King.
Nebuchadnezzar was very angry, which caused a sudden rift.
He became so furious that he promised their execution swift.

He ordered to be put to death all his advisors by decree.
But Daniel using wisdom and tact, then asked him to agree,
To allow more time to explain the dream dreamt by the King.
So they would not be executed at Nebuchadnezzar's whim.

Daniel pleaded with God in Heaven to reveal the mystery.
At night the vision and its meaning were revealed for him to see.
The King's messenger came to tell him Daniel could explain his dream.
Daniel told him all about them, and exactly what they mean.

Daniel also told the King, no-one could his dream explain,
So all his advisers and astrologers were really not to blame.
He said that it is God in Heaven who reveals all mystery.
He has shown you what will happen, in the future what will be.

"Your God is the God of gods and the Lord of all earth's kings,"
The King replied to Daniel, "for you told me all these things."
So he promoted Daniel, put him in charge of his wise men.
He rewarded his three friends and Daniel attended his court again.

Later on, Nebuchadnezzar died and was succeeded by his son.
But King Belshazzar's reign was short, for bad things he had done.
Daniel told him that God had numbered the days that he would reign.
And on that very night, the King of Babylon was slain.

Darius, the Mede, became the ruler and so began his reign.
He was so impressed with Daniel, wanted his service to retain.
The Kings advisors grew jealous, so corruption tried to find.
They hoped concerning Daniel, the King would change his mind.

They asked the King to issue an edict and enforce it by decree.
To write it down and make it law, to which Darius would agree,
That anyone who worshipped a god, or any man but him,
Would be thrown into the lions' den for committing such a sin.

As was Daniel's usual practice, he went three times a day,
Before his upstairs window, to give thanks to God and pray.
The King's advisors said, "Daniel has ignored your decree."
They called for his punishment, the King reluctant to agree.

He finally gave the order, Daniel was thrown into the den.
The King said, "May God save you, as on Him you do depend."
So he went back to his palace, but he couldn't eat or sleep.
And at the first light of dawn, he hurried quickly to his feet.

The King called in an anguished voice when to the den he came.
He was so full of joy when Daniel answered to his name.
Daniel then told the King that he'd been loyal at all times,
And that God had sent an angel to rescue him from the lions.

There are important lessons we can glean from Daniel's life;
Commitment and faith in God, kept him from harm and strife.
Honourably managing the Kings affairs, without compromise.
He always did the right thing before all men's watching eyes.

Daniel stayed ever close to God. He prayed three times a day.
If he or the King was troubled, to his God he then would pray.
He was a mighty prophet to whom the future God revealed.
Daniel always stayed humble and did not God's glory steal.

We may also suffer in this life, receive blessing and honour too.
No matter what happens to us, we should always Him pursue.
But whether in God's providence, it's our time to live or die,
We should give glory to our God, and lift His Holy Name on high.

Daniel Chs. 1–6.

THE RESURRECTION

"Our faith is in vain," the Apostle Paul said,
"If Jesus Christ hasn't been raised from the dead."
Christian faith hinges upon the resurrection.
It's important that we can make this connection.
The claim Jesus was raised, if it were not true,
Wouldn't have a lasting, effect upon you.
On the other hand, if it turns out to be true,
There's one logical thing you then need to do.

To turn from doing life your own selfish way.
Decide to let Christ's will in your life take sway.
Inviting His Spirit to come and to fill you inside,
Is possible only as He rose again when He died.
Only if Christ lives, can we have a real connection,
Walking daily with Him and enjoying His affection.
If Jesus died, was buried and stayed in the ground,
No relationship with Him could possibly be found.

If about something false we then testify,
And though untrue we choose upon it to rely,
Then for us there'll be no forgiveness for our sin,
If the One who gives it, over death did not win.
Those who've fallen asleep then really have no hope.
We can eat and drink and in our lives try to cope.
If Christ is not raised we are pitied above all men,
To have faith in Him who did not rise again.

If Christ was not raised, and the Holy Spirit revealed,
Then whose is the presence within us that we feel?
Patterns of behaviour and our natures re-arrange,
His work in our hearts, our actions He will change.
Christ was indeed raised and so dealt with our sin.
When He returns, He'll take us home to be with Him.
He was the first fruits of the living, to be followed then by men,
Who die in their faith, to eternal life will rise again.

---

1 Cor. Ch. 15.

THE RICH FOOL

Jesus told a story about a certain wealthy man.
You could say he was wise with everything well planned.
He had a bountiful harvest, his ground produced a lot.
"What shall I do?" he said, "Where will I store my crop?"

He thought about his problem, the answer came he knew.
"I'll tear down all my barns, only bigger ones will do.
I'll fill them to the brim and have plenty in reserve.
I'll eat, drink, be merry, surely this I now deserve.

I'll have plenty of good things, laid up for many years.
I'll take it easy from now on, the envy of my peers."
But God called that man a fool, himself only did he serve.
That night God called his soul, so who got what he reserved?

Wasn't he just prudent when he planned to store his grain?
Wasn't Joseph commended when He did the very same?
Was it sin to have plenty or for being well prepared?
Or was it more about how with no-one else he shared?

The most important thing, for which he had not planned,
Was his reckoning with God, when his soul God did demand.
Into an 'unholy trinity' trap he fell, of me, myself and I,
He failed to ask the question, "What will happen when I die?"

We can make the same mistake, if in wealth we feel secure,
Enticed by things we own, drawn in by their allure.
The rich man wasn't called a fool for planning or his wealth.
He spared no thought for others, was just living for himself.

Despite a blessed life, he gave God no gratitude,
Nor his workers, who planted to help his wealth accrue.
No thought of what God requires, only about me and mine.
Or that God, who gave him life, could take it back at any time.

No amount of wealth can save from accident or disease,
Nor can it stop a tragedy, which brings us to our knees.
Won't patch broken friendships or buy us any love,
And won't mend our relationship with our gracious God above.

It's not that God frowns upon us saving for our needs.
When He sees us eat and drink, He may be very pleased.
He shares His lavish bounty, things to cherish and enjoy.
He doesn't want us feeling guilt, He's not a harsh killjoy.

But we must always be aware, where true security lies,
How we invest God's gifts and how we spend our lives.
So, are our lives aligned to self and our momentary desires,
Or to God and our neighbour, which is what our Lord requires?

A person well may have regrets when at the end of life,
But he rarely says, "keep more for you," or similar advice.
We don't often hear, "I should have lived more for my own pleasure."
Living for God, our future's secure, beyond all earthly measure.

Luke 12:13–21.

THE SNAKE IN THE DESERT

Fleeing Egypt's slave masters, they were by Moses led.   1
They wandered through the desert lands after they had fled.
Pharaoh treated Israelites with contempt, and dread,   2
For whenever he oppressed them, they multiplied and spread.

He treated them so harshly, made them do much hard labour.
Not realising that these people, were under The Lord's favour.
God sent many plagues to break Pharaoh's will, and so,   3
He changed his stubborn mind and he let the people go.

"If they see war," God said, "They'll soon want to return."   4
He sent them by a safe way, so for Egypt wouldn't yearn.
He didn't lead them on the road, through Philistine country.
He took them round the desert which was close to the Red Sea.

God led in a cloud by day and a pillar of fire by night.   5
They could travel without stopping, for the fire gave them light.
But they hadn't travelled very far, were not long out of sight,
When Pharaoh changed his mind again and wished to make a fight.   6

He had his chariot made ready and his army did prepare.
The Israelites looked up to see the army almost there.
As the troops marched closer, the people were terrified.
To the Lord and to Moses, "What have you done?" they cried.

"We were better off in Egypt; we should have stayed to serve.
Why should we die in this desert, it's not what we deserve?"
But Moses wasn't left alone, God said, "Listen now to me,
Lift up your staff, stretch out your hand and I'll divide the sea."

He parted the Red Sea for them to reach the other side.
Sent manna bread from heaven and quail fell down from the sky.   7
For many years thereafter, Moses continued as their guide.
He once struck a rock for water, when their throats were dry.   8

So God provided for them, over and over again.
But despite what God delivered, they would constantly complain.
"Pharaoh was harsh," they said, "but at least we ate good fare.   9
Not this miserable food from God, which we can hardly bear."   10

So, God sent venomous snakes, among the Israelites to bite.
It didn't take long for some to die, so then they saw their plight.
"Against the Lord we have sinned," for Moses' prayers they sought.
Knowing trouble on themselves they had consequently wrought.

About the matter Moses prayed, a prayer which his God heard.
And God was quick to answer, gave instructions by His Word.
"Make a snake that all can see, raise it high upon a pole.
Those bitten can then look at it and once again be whole."

So Moses made a bronze snake, on a pole he lifted high.
Those bitten, who then looked at it, did not fall and die.
This foreshadowed something else, a "type" as it is known.   11
Pointing towards an anti-type in the future to be shown.   12

Thus recorded in God's Word many centuries later,
And better than the shadow, the anti-type is so much greater.
Jesus said, "Moses lifted the snake, to look upon and live,
So the Son of Man must be lifted up, eternal life to give."   13

Why was a bronze snake given, to look upon and live?
Surely better symbols, Moses would've had to give.
A serpent conjures evil, is an image of our sin.
Christ was the later anti-type, to live we look at Him.

All our sins were laid on Him, so God made no mistake.
Telling Moses, upon a pole, to put the symbol of a snake.
When Jesus hung upon a cross, God could not look at Him.
Because He, dying in our place, was covered in our sin.   14

Jesus cried, "God, my God, why have you forsaken me."   15
He called out in anguish, as He hung there on the tree.
And just like the serpent, lifted high for all to see.
Everyone to Christ must look, including you and me.   16

---

1. Exodus 13:17–18. 2. Exodus 1:8–14. 3. Exodus 7:14–12:30. 4. Exodus 13:17–18.
5. Exodus 13:21–22. 6. Exodus 14:5–17. 7. Exodus 16. 8. Exodus 17:1–7. 9. Exodus 16:3.
10. Numbers 21:4–9. 11. Heb. 8:5, 9:9–10, 10:1. 12. Rom 5:14, 10:1–6. 13. John 3:14–15.
14. 2 Cor. 5:21, Hab. 1:13. 15. Matt. 27:46. 16. Heb. 12:2.

THE SOWER

Jesus sat by a lake while the people gathered round.
Crowds stood on the shore but in a boat was Jesus found.
He told them many things, using parables to explain,
Shone light on truths and secrets, made them easier to retain.

Saying, "A farmer widely spread his seed, upon the open ground.
Some fell upon the path, and by the birds was found.
Some fell on rocky places, which didn't have much soil.
And because it had no root, the sun its growth did foil.

Still others fell among the thorns, and so the plants would choke.
But some fell upon good soil, giving them a better hope.
Producing a crop, so much more than actually sown.
Those with ears let them hear, the truth by them be known."

"Why do you speak in parables, can't you make it plain?"
The request from His disciples was for Jesus to explain.
"Secret knowledge of Heaven, has been given unto you.
But they refuse to believe, so won't find out what's true."

Did He wish to hide the message, and make it hard to grasp?
Or was it He could see that unbelief was in their hearts?
"The one who seeks to understand, more truth then will receive.
But what He has will be taken, from him who won't believe."

For him the parable's truth, Christ would not then reveal.
His closed ears and eyes, from him the truth would steal.
Ever hearing, not understanding, unable to perceive.
A calloused heart makes it impossible, for him to believe.

"But blessed are eyes that see and the ears that can hear.
Many prophets, righteous ones and others of their peers,
Have not seen or heard, what *you* have seen and heard."
Then Jesus said, "I'll tell you the meaning of my Words.

If anyone hears the message and does not understand.
Satan snatches from his heart, a flame that had been fanned.
This seed falls along the path, when by the farmer sown.
The evil one comes to steal his faith, before it's fully grown.

Some hear, and at once, they receive the Word with joy.
But because they have no root, their faith is easy to destroy.
This seed falls on rocky ground, when trouble comes their way,
Persecuted for their faith, they quickly fall away.

Seed that falls among thorns, is one who hears the Word,
But by the worries of this life, is choked and can't be heard.
The deceitfulness of wealth, make it fail to reproduce.
He understands the message, but can't produce the fruit.

But anyone who hears the word and truly understands.
This is seed on good soil and then a strong plant stands.
Produces a crop, yielding a hundred, sixty or thirty fold.
More than the sum of all the seeds, their numbers are untold."

Matt. Ch. 13:1–23.

THE WORD OF GOD

It was written by the hands of men,
With the Holy Spirit's prompting pen.
Now in our hands, God's Holy Word,
Is sharper than a double edged Sword.

It separates marrow from the bone,
Judges thoughts which to Him are known.
It reveals wrong attitudes of the heart.
The things from which we should depart.

Yet how do we know the Bible is true,
And has ramifications for me and you?
If we prove it's just a fallacy,
Then it has no bearing on you and me.

Well recorded facts about our history,
Are accepted and believed most readily.
Magellan existed, he lived and died,
And Isaac Newton who studied the sky.

Many others, I could mention too.
History's replete with more than a few.
But the volume of documents shared,
Is few when with the Bible compared.

The Bible's main character we can attest.
Most students of History, likewise confess.
The evidence has made this matter clear.
Jesus walked on earth, was physically here.

Tacitus and Josephus, I mention these two,
Were secular writers, a Roman and a Jew.
About a man of miracles, one of them wrote.
The other about killing Christians, did gloat.

Old Testament texts their own proofs yield.
More than three hundred prophecies, Jesus fulfilled.
Written hundreds of years before His birth.
Predicted His death and resurrection from earth.   4

Some say Jesus well the Scriptures knew.
Lived His life to fulfil prophecy too.
His birth-place the prophets did predict,   5
It's obvious by Him, couldn't be fixed.

Other evidence which forms a part,
Is the fact I have Jesus within my heart.   6
While this is difficult for me to prove,
If you accept Him, you'll know it's true.

But for me, the greatest proof of all,
Are the many transformed lives, I can recall.   7
Peace and joy in Jesus, most profound,   8
Nothing like it, in this world is found.

---

1. 2 Tim 3:16. 2. John 1:1, Ps. 119:9, Isaiah 40:8. 3. Heb. 4:12. 4. Isaiah 53:12, Ps. 16:10.
5. Micah 5:2. 6. John 14:17, Rev. 3:20. 7. 2 Cor. 5:17. 8. Gal 5:22, Phil. 4:7.

THREE CROSSES

Three crosses stood in a place called "The Skull."
A large gathering of people around Jesus did mull.
Soldiers who cast lots while dividing His clothes,
Said, "Save yourself if you're the Messiah God chose."

Two criminals alongside were paraded and led,
On each side of Jesus, as for us He bled.
A notice above Him read, "THE KING OF THE JEWS".
He prayed, "Forgive them, they know not what they do."

"Aren't you the Christ?" one, mocking, would say,
"Why not save yourself and us too today?"
"Don't you fear *God?*" the second criminal's rebuke.
That God does exist, he was most resolute.   1

That he asked the first man, "God … *don't you fear?*"   2
Showed he knew that for them, a reckoning was near.   3
"We'll get what we deserve for our wrongful deeds."   4
So admitting that *Just* was the punishment *they* received. 5

Looking at Jesus, "This man's done no wrong."
Here in His innocence, He did not belong.   6
He then asked Him, "When into your Kingdom you come,
Please remember me," sensing He was *God's Son.*   7

He understood that Jesus was the one authority,   8
Who could grant his request, He was the vital key.   9
Knowing his heart Jesus said, "The truth I tell,   10
Today I'll be in paradise, you'll be with me as well.

Luke 23:32–43. **1.** Heb. 11:6. **2.** Prov. 9:10. **3.** Heb. 9:27. **4.** Rom. 3:23. **5.** Rom. 6:23.
6. 1 Peter 3:18. **7.** Luke 9:20. **8.** John 1:12. **9.** Heb. 12:2. **10.** Rom. 10:10.

THREE STORIES

There were three parables, which once Jesus told.
Though each somewhat different, a central message would unfold.
They tell us just how far God is prepared to go,
To find His lost children, and them for Him to know.
There were two groups of people whom Jesus addressed.
Tax collectors and sinners, who all their sins confessed.
Then to the Pharisees, who stuck out their chests,
Who were also sinners, but good works they professed.

Jesus said, "Suppose one of you, had a hundred sheep,
Then you lost one, which you really wished to keep.
Wouldn't you straightway leave the ninety-nine behind,
And embark on a search, until the lost one you could find?
You would call your friends together, your joy with them to share,
To help you celebrate, that your once lost sheep was there.
There's more rejoicing in Heaven, over a sinner who is found,
Than ninety-nine righteous ones, already heaven bound."

And then, a lost coin story Jesus also wished to tell.
A very careful hunt was made, a house swept really well.
Ten silver coins this woman had, but sadly she lost one.
She trimmed and lit a lamp, her thorough search had just begun.
Yes! She found the lost piece, she'd been searching for some time,
Told her friends, "I found again, the coin that once was mine."
She asked them to rejoice in her happiness that day.
And rejoicing in heaven, happens the very same way.

The third story He told, about a most ungrateful son.
Asked His Father to give him his whole inheritance fund.
He spent it very quickly, impoverished then became.
Was in a far-off country, without a penny to his name.
When he came to his senses, to home he then returned,
Knowing his family ties were well and truly burned.
Yet his Father who loved him, saw him coming from afar,
And threw his arms around him, the relationship unmarred.

So once again, of course, there was a happy celebration.
The father just could not contain, or hide, his jubilation.
He ordered a fattened calf, by his servants to be killed.
Rejoiced with his workers, their stomachs all well filled.
Our heavenly Father searches, and for us He calmly waits,
For the ones who are lost, He wants to celebrate.
With His arms open wide, He will long for us and yearn.
And all of Heaven rejoices, when His own loved ones return.

Luke Ch. 15.

TWO ROADS – ONE WAY

As I travel along life's highway.
There are many choices and many roads.
But I know to whom I'll surrender.
It is the only way for me to go.
There is one way to the Father.   1
Only one way, through the Son.
Yes, but one way to the Father,
Through the work that He has done.   2

They say that all roads lead to Heaven.
It doesn't matter which way you go.
You can follow Buddha or Mohammed,
Hari Krishna, but this I know,
There is one way to the Father.
Only one way, through the Son.
Yes, but one way to the Father,
Through the work that He has done.

There are two roads on life's journey,   3
One is narrow and one is wide.
If you wonder which one to follow,
Jesus showed us when He died.
There is one way to the Father.
Only one way, through the Son.
Yes, but one way to the Father,
Through the work that He has done.

---

1. John 14:6. **2.** 1 Pet. 3:18. **3.** Matt. 7:13–14.

UPON THIS ROCK
THE APOSTLE PETER

Who Jesus was caused great debate among the Jews.
His claim to be God, they just could not excuse.
Pharisees and Sadducees came to put Him to the test.
Jesus listened patiently to all of their requests.
He lost patience with them, when they asked Him for a sign,
So departing from the Jews, their invitation he declined.
Joining His disciples this question He put to them,
"Who do people say that I, the Son of Man, am?"

They mentioned various prophets, so Jesus said again,
"But, now I'm asking you, who do *you* say I am?"
Ever impetuous, Peter didn't need another prod.
He said, "You are the Christ, Son of the living God."
Jesus said, "Flesh and blood didn't make this known to you.
My Father in Heaven did, and this is how you knew.
You are Peter, and I'll build my church upon this rock.
The very gates of Hades, won't prevail against my flock."

After Jesus rose, the disciples all went to Jerusalem.
For the Holy Spirit waited, as Jesus had promised them.
Suddenly a sound, like a blowing mighty gale,
Came rushing down from Heaven, the whole house did assail.
They saw there what appeared to be separate tongues of fire,
But were not fully aware of what would then transpire.
The fire rested on them and being Holy Spirit filled,
They spoke in other languages, Joel's prophesy revealed. 1

Now God-fearing Jews from every nation under Heaven,
Gathered around Peter, as well as the Eleven.
Hearing the violent wind, and attracted by the sound,
Each heard their own language, them did utterly astound.
They were all amazed, for Galileans were they, who spoke.
Others thinking they were drunk, much fun at them did poke.
Peter stood up to speak, and to address the crowd,
Explaining they were not drunk, as he raised his voice aloud.

He told them Jesus Christ, whom they had crucified.
Was raised by God to life again, after He had died.
Old Testament truths, he went on and continued to expound.
At God's right hand, Jesus, the Christ, could now be found.
When the people heard this news, they were cut right to the heart.
Peter told them to repent, and from their sins depart.
"Be baptised and the promised Holy Spirit you'll receive.
This promise is for you and all, who in Jesus Christ believe."

Peter was God's instrument, for the Church to be born.
The Apostles, in the Spirit, signs and wonders did perform.
About three thousand souls were added to them that day.
They devoted to the teaching of the Apostles, and to pray.
Fellowshipping in their homes and breaking of the bread.
Selling their possessions, they all with each other shared.
Eating together, praising God, with sincere, glad hearts.
The Lord added daily to those, salvation did impart.

Matt. Ch. 16, Acts Ch. 2. 1. Joel 2:28.

UPON THIS ROCK
THE SAMARITANS

After the birth of the Church, it fast began to grow.
Leaders were required, so things could smoothly flow.   1
Widows received no food and so a dispute arose.
To take on this duty, seven men, the people chose.
They were full of the Spirit and Phillip was one of them.
A gifted evangelist, who preached to Samaritans.
The Assyrians captured Samaria, six hundred years before.
Thousands of the Jews deported, leaving only the poor.

Soon came many pagans, who travelled from afar,
And intermarried with poor Jews … a population marred.
Samaritans were hated, frowned upon by all pure Jews.
Who considered they were half-breeds, so them they would abuse.
Phillip went down to Samaria, as he no conflict felt.   2
No racism was in his heart, for with it God had dealt.
He preached about salvation to all the people there.
With miracles, signs and wonders, the gospel he did share.

When the Samaritans heard the gospel, they received it with much joy.
Many were healed, as Phillip did the Holy Spirit employ.
In Samaria Jesus had before, sown seed and it took root.
So Phillip preached Jesus Christ and now he reaped the fruit.
Phillip baptised many of them, as soon as they believed.
All those who professed their faith, eternal life received.
But persecution of Christians was rife in Jerusalem.
Much sorrow, scorn and pain were inflicted upon them.

News reached the apostles, the Samaritans had now heard,
The message Phillip preached, and they believed in the Word.
So, Peter and John came down, for the Samaritans to pray.
Making haste, to impart the Holy Spirit straight away.
The Lord had given Peter, the Kingdom of Heaven's key,   3
To open faith's door in Christ, those bound from sin set free.
When He said, "Peter, I'll build my church upon this rock."
God helped him to explain the truth, salvation to unlock.

Jesus had told the disciples, the Holy Spirit He would send,   4
When He would rise from death, and return to heaven again.
The Holy Spirit fell on Jews who believed at Pentecost.   5
The birth of Christ's church, from those who once were lost.
Now the Samaritans too believed, and had been born again.
And just like back at Pentecost, the Holy Spirit fell on them.   6
Not only Jews but Samaritans, the Lord had come to know.
And the church kept on expanding, and continuing to grow.

---

1. Acts 6:1-4. 2. Acts 8:1–17. 3. Matt. 16:13–20. 4. John 16:7. 5. Acts 2:3–4.
6. Acts 8:16.

UPON THIS ROCK
CORNELIUS

The Lord used Simon Peter to open the Kingdom to the Jews.
To bring salvation to the Gentiles, he also did God choose.
A Roman commander, "Cornelius," who was quite well known,
Was devout and God-fearing, this he had always shown.
He was generous to the poor, for them he often prayed,
Received a vision of an angel, who to him a visit paid.
"What is it Lord?" Cornelius asked, as he stared in fear.
"Your gifts and prayer offerings, before God did appear."

The angel said, "Send men to Joppa and bring back a man,
Whose name is Simon Peter, he is part of God's great plan."
As they approached the city, it was noon of the next day,
Peter went up to the roof, to be alone and to pray.
He became very hungry and while a meal was being made,
Peter fell into a trance, while fervently he prayed.
He saw Heaven open, something dropped down like a sheet,
With many kinds of animals … some he would never eat.

There were four footed animals and reptiles and some birds.
In wonder he looked at these and then a voice he heard.
It said for him to kill and eat, "Surely not," he then replied.
"I've never eaten unclean meat, it can't be justified."
The voice spoke a second time, the truth for him to glean.
"Do not call food impure, that God has now made clean."
Three times Simon Peter, this same vision observed.
He needed repetition so God's voice was clearly heard.

Peter wondered what the vision could be interpreted to mean,
When three men sent by Cornelius arrived upon the scene.
Still thinking on the vision, the Spirit said to him,
"Peter, men are looking for you, go down and let them in."
So, he went down to tell them, "I'm the one you're looking for."
They told of Cornelius' vision, which he could simply not ignore.
"You must come to his house, he will hear what you have to say."
So, Peter went to Joppa, it was on the following day.

The truth about the vision that finally dawned on him,
Was, God wants to save the Gentiles also, from their sin.
The vision was about people, nothing to do with food,
It was the message of the Gospel, God wants all men to include.
Cornelius, expecting them, had invited some close friends,
To hear Peter's message, the one whom God did send.
A large gathering was there that he did not expect to find,
So he explained that God had opened his eyes that once were blind.

He told them, "In the law, a Jew can't mix with a Gentile.
But God said we mustn't call anyone, unclean or defiled.
I now realise it's true," he said, "no favouritism God will show.
Peace comes through Jesus Christ, all men He wants to know."
So, Peter recalled history, how Jesus lived, died and rose.
How He had appeared to them, whom God beforehand chose.
That God anointed Jesus, with the Holy Spirit's power,
Healings, many miracles and love on them he showered.

He said, "We are witnesses of all He said and did."
Told them that to follow Him, the Pharisees forbid.
"They killed Jesus, when to the cross, they had Him nailed.
But their plans to dispose of Him, all completely failed.
For upon the third day, God raised Him from the dead.
He was seen by witnesses, and by us as well," he said.
"All who believe in Him receive forgiveness in His Name."
And while Peter was still speaking, the Holy Spirit came.

He filled all those present, the Jews with Peter were amazed.
They heard them speak in tongues, as our God they praised.
Peter ordered their baptism, no-one stood in their way.
The Gentiles then asked Peter, if for some days he could stay.
So the church kept on expanding and continuing to grow.
The Gentiles now invited in, for God His love to show.
We're forgiven if with all our hearts, for Christ we make a search.   1
Upon the rock of Peter, Jesus Christ would build His church.

Acts Ch. 10. 1. Jeremiah 29:13.

UPON THIS ROCK
THE APOSTLE PAUL

There was a man, Spirit filled, and Stephen was his name.   1
Before the Sanhedrin, Jews brought him to lay blame.   2
To this Jewish council, Stephen did explain,
They killed their own prophets, so they should feel much shame.   3
They flouted their own laws, just like their fathers did.
To speak about the righteous One, they also did forbid.
Killed those who predicted, that He was to come.
Betrayed and murdered Him, who was God's only Son.

When Stephen looked up, he saw Christ at God's right hand.
The Jews blocked their ears, what he said they couldn't stand.
So, they began to stone him and as they watched him fall.
Laid their clothes at the feet of a man whose name was Saul.   4
Saul, was a religious man, who for God was full of zeal.   5
He persecuted Christians, hunted them down to kill.
A Hebrew of the Hebrews, lack of strictness did abhor.   6
Circumcised on the eighth day, according to the law.

Of Israel's stock and heir to God's covenant with them.
Israel's first king came from his tribe of Benjamin.
Of the elite sect of Pharisees, to keep the law was their aim.
Righteousness according to law, no-one could lay blame.
What would it take to turn around, a mind and will so strong?
A zealot who was most sincere, but most sincerely wrong.
He hauled believers off to prison, almost every other day.   7
Made murderous threats to Christians, the people of the "Way."

On a journey to Damascus, from Heaven came a sound.   8
Blinding light flashed round him as he fell down on the ground.
Then a voice he heard said, "Saul, why do you mistreat me?"
The men with Saul stood speechless, Saul could no longer see.
"Who are you Lord?" Saul asked. The voice said, "I am He,
The one you've persecuted, now that will cease to be.
Stand up, go to the city," but because Saul was then blind,
They helped him up and led him, his own way couldn't find.

Saul was very hungry, he hadn't eaten for three days.
Saw Ananias in a vision, when to the Lord he prayed.
Jesus said he would tell Saul, exactly what to do.
And to His disciple, Ananias, Jesus gave a vision too.
"To the house of Judas go, you'll find it on Straight Street.
 A man from Tarsus, 'Saul', you are going there to meet.
Place your hands upon him and restore to him his sight."
He knew Saul's reputation so objected in much fright.

"He's my chosen instrument," Jesus said, "so you must go.
How he must suffer for my name, he'll surely come to know.   9
To the people of Israel, and to Gentiles, he'll take my name."
Ananias left straight away and to the house of Judas came.
Placing hands upon Saul's head, his blindness then to heal.
As scales fell from Saul's eyes, with the Spirit he was filled.
He took some food, was baptised and once again was strong.
He'd preach about the Lord now, to Him, he would belong.

Saul, also known as Paul, didn't visit former peers.   10
Went to the Arabian Desert, for round about three years.
His Gospel was not learned from the Apostles or anyone else.
Paul received direct revelation, from Jesus Christ Himself.
He then went to Jerusalem, Apostle Peter he wished to see.
He also met with James, and preached Christ fearlessly.
He mainly preached to Gentiles, but to Jew and Gentile both.
Through the then-known world, the church saw massive growth.

On Paul's mission of the gospel, he suffered for the Lord.   11
Later on would die for Him, but was faithful to the Word.
Into salvation's message, his whole being he then poured.   12
He counted all things but loss, for the sake of Heaven's reward.   13
His life stands as a lesson, from which you and I can learn.
The gospel which Paul preached, is something we can't earn.   14
We are not found in Christ, with righteousness of our own.
In righteousness from faith in Him, we find our Heavenly home.

---

1. Acts 6: 8. 2. Acts 6: 12. 3. Acts 7: 51–59. 4. Acts 7:58. 5. Acts 9:1–2. 6. Phil. 3:4–6.
7. Acts 9:1–3. 8. Acts 9:3–20. 9. Acts 9:16. 10. Gal. 1:11–19. 11. 1 Cor. 4:12.
12. 2 Cor. 11:22–28, 2 Cor. 4:9. 13. Phil. 3:8. 14. Phil. 3:9.

UPON THIS ROCK
THE PERSECUTED CHURCH

From very small beginnings, the church of God, it grew.   1
From the very outset, opposition strong, it knew.   2
As Stephen opposed the Jews, they cruelly stoned him dead.   3
Christians were persecuted, when the Gospel they had spread.
The Pharisees and Jews, had put Jesus Christ to death,   4
But mistakenly thought that they had silenced the threat.
Didn't think His followers, who were mostly timid men,   5
Fearlessly would resurrect His message, once again.   6

Their total transformation, wasn't what they did expect.
About their message, Sadducees were really quite upset.   7
They taught that in Jesus, there's a rising of the dead.   8
So they seized John and Peter and wanted their blood shed.
Peter and John went to the temple at the time of prayer.
A crippled man, from birth, received their healing there.   9
The Sadducees were jealous, this was the final straw.   10
Jesus' teachings were now becoming popular once more.

Christian numbers growing, began to cause them stress.
So they threw them into jail, until the problem could assess.
Peter and John were threatened, but they finally let them go.
The spreading of their message, they tried desperately to slow.
The Apostles kept on preaching and many more did heal.
The high Priest rose in anger, for their message had appeal.   11
Took hold of the Apostles and to prison they went again.
And next morning took the matter, before the Sanhedrin.

But the night before, an angel, the Apostles he released.
They went straight to the temple, their teaching hadn't ceased.
Officers went to fetch them, to again the leaders face.
So, Peter and the Apostles, then boldly made their case.
The Leaders said, "We've told you, do not teach in that Name?
But because you won't obey, you're in front of us again."
They said, "We will obey God, rather than obey men."
A teacher of the law, "Gamaliel," then chose to intervene.

He said, "Men of Israel, calmly consider what you'll do.
Men have risen in the past, and drawn a following too.
They all came to nought, before their work became full blown.
It's best to keep your distance, and leave these men alone.
For if their plans are 'of men', they'll come to nothing too,
But if they're found to be 'of God', there's nothing we can do."
His logic was persuasive, so the Apostles were released,
Soundly beaten, and warned that their teaching must now cease.

They never did stop preaching, the message of Good News,
That Jesus is the Christ, and for salvation, Him we choose.
After Stephen's stoning, more persecution harmed the Church.   12
Many Christians were scattered, but they weren't left in the lurch.
While spreading forth the gospel, the Spirit's power they employed.   13
But Saul a zealous Jew arose, to have the church destroyed.   14
There were many at that time, who the church, did persecute.
But Saul was most successful, for his goals were resolute.

Then his life was turned around on that Damascus road.
His crusade to kill Christians, would suddenly implode.
He heard a voice from Heaven, was surrounded by a light,
And needed help to travel on, because he lost his sight.
Saul, also called Paul, followed Christ that very day.
No longer captured Christians, the people of the "Way."
Persecutor was persecuted, in the blinking of an eye.
Fearlessly preached the gospel, "Follow Jesus," was his cry.

Suffering much persecution he was martyred for his faith.   15
A better reward in Heaven, for the faithful there awaits.   16
Throughout all of History, a persecuted church we find,
But to the battle's real enemy, Christians are not blind.
From the very beginning, Satan's played a definite role:
Defeated at the cross, he wants to wrestle back control.   17
So oppression will continue, the mighty battle rages on.
Not till we reach Heaven, will afflictions be forever gone.   18

The more pain and suffering the church must undergo,   19
The more new seeds will sprout, and the more the church will grow.
Many times in our world, this pattern will repeat.
Gamaliel's true words echo, "If of God, we can't defeat."   20
God created laws of nature, which we already know.
We must always prune the plant, if we want a tree to grow.
So as Christians, with joy we look our battles in the face,
And when at last in Heaven we stand, we will not see disgrace.   21

Persecution may increase, and never go away.   22
'That we remain faithful, no matter what,' is how we pray.   23
May you faithfully endure, daily taking up your cross,   24
And for the joy set before you, count everything but loss.   25
Despite trials of your faith, determine to follow our Lord.   26
Trials of this life pale, compared to Heavenly reward.   27
A battle is waged in Heavenly realms, for your eternal soul.   28
Will you fully yield to Christ or bend to Satan's control?

---

1. Acts 2:47. 2. Acts 5:17. 3. Acts 7:59. 4. Matt. 27:45–50. 5. Matt. 26:58. 6. Acts 4:13.
7. Acts 4:2. 8. Acts 4:2–3. 9. Acts 3:1–10. 10. Acts 4:1–21. 11. Acts 5:17–42.
12. Acts 8:1–4. 13. Acts 8:6–8. 14. Acts 9:1–19. 15. 2 Cor. 11:23–30. 16. 1 Cor. 2:9.
17. Rom. 16:20, Heb. 2:14. 18. Rev. 21:4. 19. Matt. 24:9, 2 Tim. 3:1. 20. Acts 5:38–39.
21. Matt. 25:13, 34. 22. Matt. 5:10, 2 Tim 3:12. 23. Matt 24:13. 24. Luke 9:23.
25. Phil 3:8. 26. James 1:12. 27. Matt. 5:12. 28. Rev. 12:17.

UPON THIS ROCK
CHURCH PICTURES

God's Word is living and active, and Holy Spirit breathed. 1
The Church a living organism, from Christ to us bequeathed. 2
"Ecclesia," the 'called out' ones, are all those born again. 3
The Holy Spirit supplies God's love, on which she does depend. 4
She is God's community, who faith in Christ express, 5
And she is not a building, but those, Christ does possess. 6
Church is something that we *are*, not something that we *do*,
So, if we truly know the Lord, the Church is *me* and *you*. 7

Born of life, formed of life, and through whom Jesus lives. 8
Her life breathed by the Spirit, whom Jesus freely gives. 9
The Church is now worldwide, to God's praise and acclaim. 10
She exists whenever two or three are gathered in His Name. 11
Jesus says that He is with us, whenever His people meet. 12
The Church without His presence, can never be complete. 13
His presence is always with us, when we share the bread and wine, 14
And Him we all remember, when we take them, every time. 15

God's word portrays the Church, with powerful metaphors.
Body of Christ, Family of God, and there are many more …
His Kingdom, The Bride of Christ, that's just to name a few.
God's House, a Field, a Vineyard, and God's Temple too.
Paul says our Human Body, reveals clearly and describes,
Her unique design and structure, which he, to Christ, ascribes. 16
She's made up of many members, yet *many* still form *one*. 17
No course can she chart, without her "Head," who is God's Son. 18

Her members have a role to play, they are uniquely made,   19
Natural talent and Spirit's gifting, in each of them displayed.   20
The parts all work together, in perfect love and harmony.   21
Just like members of the bodies, which belong to you and me.   22
So, if one suffers all will suffer, if one is blessed, all rejoice.   23
Constantly sharing in God's Word, listening to the Spirit's voice.   24
When all members work together, a healthy Church can grow.   25
New members, born again, added, as Christ they come to know.   26

The Church, the Bride of Christ, this picture is portrayed.   27
A pure, unblemished bride, a righteous virgin she is made.   28
Allowed to clothe herself with linen, fine and bright and pure.   29
No righteousness of her own, for Christ Himself, it did secure.   30
A man will leave his parents and with his wife become one flesh.   31
This mystery is profound and a union God will bless.
For these words to Christ refer, show the union we have in Him.
We will united be as one, and cleansed despite our sin.   32

God's Church is a Family, as sons and daughters we belong.   33
And so as family members, we seek to keep each other strong.   34
We are members of God's household and siblings to each other,   35
Growing close relationships, praying for sister and brother.   36
The Church is the Temple of God, which is built with living stones.   37
Apostles and Prophets are its foundation, the temple that Jesus owns.   38
And Christ is the cornerstone, on which the building rests,   39
Despite Him being the very stone, the people did reject.   40

If we remove the cornerstone, the building would collapse,   41
But in Christ the building is secure, so we won't see it lapse.
As we are individual stones and part of the temple form.   42
The Holy Spirit in us dwells for our duties to perform.
So, Church is so much more, than a place that we attend,
Where we go to only once a week, and together one hour spend.
Christ builds us up together, into a continual dwelling place,   43
Where God lives by His Spirit and fills the temple by His grace.

---

1. Heb. 4:12. 2. 1 Cor. 12:27. 3. 1 Pet. 2:9. 4. Rom. 5:5. 5. Rom 10:9. 6. Rom 8:9.
7. Eph. 5:30. 8. Acts 2:2–4, 17:24–28. 9. John 14:16, 1 Cor. 3:16. 10. Matt. 24:14.
11. Matt. 18:20. 12. Matt. 28:20, Rom. 8:10, 2 Cor. 13:5. 13. John 15:4.
14. 1 Cor. 10. 16–17. 15. 1 Cor. 11:26. 16. Rom 12:4–5. 17. 1 Cor. 10:17. 18. Col 1:18.
19. 1 Cor. 12:12. 20. Rom. 12:6–8. 21. Eph. 4:15–16. 22. Rom. 12:4. 23. 1 Cor. 12:26.
24. Mark 13:11, 2 Tim. 2:15. 25. Eph. 4:16. 26. Acts 2:47, 1 Pet. 2:5. 27. Rev. 21:9.
28. Eph. 5:27. 29. Rev 19:7–8. 30. Phil 3:9. 31. Eph. 5:31–32. 32. Rev.22:17.
33. 2 Cor. 6:18. 34. 1 Thess. 5:11. 35. Eph. 2:19. 36. Eph. 6:18. 37. 1 Pet. 2:5.
38. 1 Cor. 3:10–11. 39. Eph. 2:20. 40. 1 Pet. 2:6–7. 41. Eph. 2:20–21.
42. 2 Tim. 1:14, 1 Pet. 2:5. 43. Eph. 2:19–22.

UPON THIS ROCK
THE REMNANT

"Hear oh heavens, listen oh earth," did the prophet Isaiah say,
As he recalled his vision of what God said to him that day.
"Unless God left a remnant then we could well have been,
Like Sodom and Gomorrah, taken away from this earth's scene."   1
The question may well be asked, "What does a remnant mean?"
A little piece left over, part of a larger piece it's been.
A small group of people, piece of material or a carpet scrap,
Or after a great calamity, those left in the aftermath.

Only highly prized by him who can't pay much.
To God is highly valued, He has the remnant in His clutch.   2
God speaks of a remnant and never gives up on them.   3
Their number may be small, but they He does intend,
To carry forth His banner and tell of His great works.   4
He's always calling out to them, never gives up His search.   5
In God's dealing with the remnant He may both judge and bless.   6
At times allowing tragedy when sins they should confess.   7

Around Six Hundred BC, the Babylonians to Judah came,   8
Killed many Jews, took captives, but a remnant did remain.   9
A remnant returned much later, to re-build the city wall.   10
They were led by Nehemiah, who responded to God's call.
Only Lot and his daughters survived Sodom and Gomorrah.   11
Many other times a remnant withstood all kinds of horror.
When Israel bowed to idols and to worship God, they failed,   12
He reserved a remnant who did not bow down to Baal.

Abraham's offspring, God said, will be countless as sea sand.   13
In the last days they'll see salvation, but only a remnant will stand.   14
For Jew and Gentile both together, God's promises will mesh.   15
The remnant, 'according to promise,' not to heirs of the flesh.   16
Paul mentioned a remnant, not of works, but chosen just by grace,   17
Based solely on the righteousness, which only comes by faith.   18
He was unashamed of the Gospel because of all that it could do,
God's power for the salvation of the Gentile and the Jew.   19

The remnant … the Church's Body of true Christians everywhere.   20
They are loyal to their Lord, and in His sufferings they share.   21
The prophetic Word of God says that the time is now at hand.   22
Jesus declares a blessing on him who reads and understands.   23
Satan often deceives the world, but the remnant can't delude.   24
He prowls like a roaring lion, and with Christians wars and feuds.   25
The remnant enters the narrow gate, found only by a few.   26
But broad is destruction's road, I pray not found by you.

---

1. Isaiah 1:9. 2. John 10:27–30. 3. Heb. 13:5. 4. Ps. 20:5, 105:2. 5. Luke 15:11–32.
6. Isaiah 17:3, Amos 5:15. 7. Micah 7:18, Heb. 12:5–8. 8. Ezra 9:8. 9. 2 Kings 24:14.
10. Neh. 3:1. 11. Gen. 19:30. 12. 1 Kings 19:18. 13. Gen. 22:17. 14. Rev. 14:12.
15. Rom. 4:16. 16. John 1:13, Rom. 11:5. 17. Rom. 11:5. 18. Gal. 3:6–14. 19. Rom. 1:16.
20. Joel 2:28–32. 21. 1 Pet. 4:13, Phil. 3:10. 22. Rev. 22:10. 23. Rev. 1:3, 2 Pet. 1:19–20.
24. Matt 24:11–15. 25. Rev. 12:17, 1 Pet. 5:8. 26. Matt. 7:13–14.

WHAT IS SIN?

It's quite an old fashioned word, but what does it really mean?
Was used by old time preachers, we're glad they're now not seen.
That "sin" word is not one that we like to talk about these days.
Maybe better not to mention it, just one another praise.

For positive words help self-esteem, it's a better way to go.
We need not be reminded of our failings that we know.
But God's Word mentions sin over four hundred times,
So it must be a real problem, that sin of yours and mine.

Just because sin's not mentioned, doesn't mean that sin's not done.
And if we do life on God's terms, He doesn't take away our fun.
Things are often polar opposites, when we're in God's economy.
The more we try to please ourselves, the more unhappy we'll be.

Let's define what we mean, there are "Sins" and there's "Sin."
"Sins" wrong actions that we do, "Sin" the state that we're born in. 1
So things we do against God's law, are symptoms of our state. 2
They are actions which the Lord says, that He does truly hate. 3

They stem from Adam's curse, with a sinful nature we are born. 4
We cannot live a perfect life, that's why our souls are torn. 5
We set ourselves some lofty goals, on good works we embark. 6
No matter just how much we try, we fall short of the mark. 7

So why should we really care if we can never get things right?
We beat ourselves up to impress our God, putting up a valiant fight.
Why not just love sin's dabbles and enjoy what we want to do? 8
Well, there are some good reasons and I'll give you just a few.

Sins give instant gratification, but have a longer lasting kick.   9
They can cripple our minds, even make us physically sick.   10
Sinning isn't good for you, it's not the way your soul was built.
God made you with a conscience, that's why you feel such guilt.   11

Sins can lead to desperation, cause your soul to seek to kill,
That empty, hollow feeling with anything that you can fill.
So-called pleasure promises much, but in the end your soul will die.   12
You can reach the place of no return when you no longer try.

Satan puts desire before you, his plan to you destroy.   13
Cunning strategies to wreck your soul, the devil will employ.   14
He uses sex, power and money, and every imaginable tool.
False promises of happiness and plays you for a fool.   15

Sins can be addictive, you can end up as their slave.   16
Then you'll find you cannot stop, or control how you behave.   17
When you follow any being and choose them to obey,   18
You then become their slave, just like the devil's prey.

We have many partners in our crimes for everyone does sin.   19
The bad news is the penalty, the reward we surely win.   20
The penalty is our own soul's death, now and through eternity.   21
The good news is that God sent Christ, to set the prisoner free.   22

Christ Jesus paid the price, died for your sins and for mine.   23
An act of grace that could only be paid by a loving God divine.   24
We can now be made fully whole, with His righteousness, not ours,   25
By His grace, and through our faith, and by the Holy Spirit's power.   26

Because of Jesus' sacrifice, from sin's penalty we're free.   27

He helps us conquer sin, His Spirit lives in you and me.   28

God gives us a new heart, upon which He writes His law.   29

We no longer desire to sin now, nor want to grieve Him anymore.   30

Now through faith, and His by grace, God's forgiven me and you.   31

We have the power of His Spirit, to forgive other people too.   32

And though we're far from perfect we're forgiven just the same.   33

Jesus, before God, is our advocate and that is why He came.   34

---

1. Ps. 51:5. **2.** Rom 7:19. **3.** Prov. 6:16-19, Rev. 2:6. **4.** Rom. 5:12. **5.** Gal. 6:7–8.
6. Eph. 2:9. **7.** Rom. 3:23. **8.** James 4:4. **9.** Ezek. 18:4. **10.** Ps. 32:3, Ps. 38, Luke 13:16, 1 Cor. 11:28–30. **11.** Rom. 2:15, Heb. 10:22. **12.** Gen. 3. **13.** 1 Pet. 5:8.
14. Gen. 3:4, 2 Cor. 2:11, 4:4, Eph. 2:2. **15.** John 8:44. **16.** Rom. 6:16.
17. Eph. 5:18, 1 Pet. 5:8. **18.** Rom. 6:16. **19.** Rom. 3:23. **20.** Rom. 6:23.
21. Ez. 18:20, 2 Thess. 1:9. **22.** Luke 4:18. **23.** 1 Cor. 6:20. **24.** Eph. 2:8, Rom. 5:8.
25. 2 Cor. 5:21. **26.** Eph. 1:13. **27.** Rom. 3:21–24. **28.** Gal. 5:16.
29. Ez. 36:26, Heb. 10:16. **30.** Prov. 8:13, Rom. 12:9, Eph. 4:30. **31.** Eph. 2:8.
32. Eph. 4:32. **33.** Heb. 8:12. **34.** 1 John 2:1.

WHAT SHOULD A MOTHER BE?

Is there anyone in life more important than a mother?
The one who gave you birth, and with love you did smother.
Held you close, clothed you, and fed you with the milk of life.
She kept you far away from harm and every other strife.
I know such a mother who is all that she should be,
Because that lovely mother is a mother to me.

And under her protection a baby is nurtured and grows.
To come between a mother and baby everybody knows.
That either brave or foolish, would that person be.
She will defend her child to death, you surely would agree.
I know such a mother who is all that she should be.
Because that lovely mother is a mother to me.

When a child grows even more and then becomes a teen.
He may not understand how strong a mother's love has been.
He can take her love for granted in his wild and wandering ways,
But an ever faithful mother drops to her knees and prays.
I know such a mother who is all that she should be,
Because that lovely mother is a mother to me.

Sometimes a mother prays for hours upon bended knees.
She humbly comes before her God as for her child she pleads.
How desperate are her utterings, our souls know very well.
She prays that God would spare her child who into trouble fell.
I know such a mother who is all that she should be'
Because that lovely mother is a mother to me.

A mother has so many noble traits, an endearing quality.
Speaking words of wisdom clothed in strength and dignity.
Kind words are on her tongue as comfort she provides.
And as a child becomes a man, she continues him to guide.
I know such a mother who is all that she should be,
Because that lovely mother is a mother to me.

When a mother has faithfully given a lifetime of her best,
Her children will rise up and declare that she is blessed.
In old age she can praise her God for a loving family,
And can leave this earth knowing that she's left a legacy.
I know such a mother who is all that she should be,
Because that lovely mother is a mother to me.

Ex. 2:6. Deut. 5:16. Prov. 1:8, 6:20, 23:22–25, 31:25–30. Isaiah 66:13. John 19:26-27.
Eph. 6:2. 2 Tim. 1:5.

WHY IS IT SO?

If I pointed my finger, in any direction that I chose.
If I could travel to its end, to find out where it goes.
After many light years pass, would I bump into a wall?
On the other side of it, what on me would then befall?

Would I see the start of other worlds or nothing there at all?
And if I could travel on again, would I find another wall?
Are there many universes, inside a grain of sand,
Among trillions of other grains, in an undiscovered land?

Can someone have forever been, and forever they will be?
If they had a beginning, who before them would we see?
If the future had an end, so that all we knew would stop.
Would nothing then come after the mighty curtain drop?

Do we even exist, or are we part of someone's thoughts?
Perhaps I imagine hurt, and the pain in me it's wrought?
These things have been debated at many different times.
By men who were so brilliant, by some of our greatest minds.

There may be many dimensions and we only live in one,
Or many planets like our earth, each having their own sun.
How do we think the earth began, did it simply evolve,
Or come from a big bang? And what problem does that solve?

Where did matter come from, before it could explode?
To understand the answer, puts our brains in overload.
For matter to exist, from something must have come.
A recent theory is from nothing, matter has begun.

Scientists study nature and behaviour of natural things.
Often proving theories, knowledge and clarity it brings.
Science is very useful, though there's still some unfilled holes.
Observation of what God has made and what He still controls.   1

So, that brings us then to God and what is spoken in His Word.
He's revealed in creation, His voice by generations heard.   2
Scripture says the universe was formed by His command.   3
From things unseen He formed it, just as He had planned.

God's Word says in the beginning, He simply did create.   4
From the Bible's perspective, there's not even a debate.
It's stated as a fact, as though all men would surely know.
God said, "Let there be," His Word's power He did show.   5

He's the alpha and omega, the beginning and the end.   6
I choose to put my faith in Him, and on Him to depend.   7
We all put faith in something, but how solid will it stand?   8
I put my faith in someone, who the universe has planned.

We can all go round and round and have a circular debate.
And back to where we began, some still won't know their fate.
If we take the smartest people, with the very brightest minds,
Even they cannot agree and common ground can't find.

Mere foolishness to God, the wisest, wisdom of mankind.   9
In comparison to Him, man walks around completely blind.
For His omniscient mind, is on a vastly higher plane.   10
Things He need not pay a mind to, will tax man's finest brain.

If intelligence is limited, reasoned debate won't suffice.
We might as well decide all things, on the rolling of a dice.
But if belief in God requires, that we exercise our faith.   11
It doesn't mean that it's not resting on a factual base.

God has provided nature and historical facts to believe.   12
We need not know all the facts, before Him we receive.
Don't need to see and understand our every circumstance,
To know that God exists, and He makes my soul to dance.   13

My soul is fed the bread of life and joyfully it sings.   14
And to drink His living water, satisfaction surely brings.   15
So if by faith you seek Him, you'll find him in your strife.
Through Jesus' precious Words, "I am the Way, the Truth, the Life."   16

---

1. Col. 1:16–17. 2. Romans 1:20. 3. Heb. 11:3. 4. Gen. 1:1. 5. Gen 1:3.
6. Isaiah 44:6, Rev.1:8. 7. Ps. 62:5-8. 8. Ps. 62:11, Prov. 18:10, 2 Tim. 1:7. 9. 1 Cor. 3:19.
10. Isaiah 55:8–9. 11. Luke 7:50. 12. Rom.1:20. 13. Heb. 11:6. 14. John 6:35.
15. John 4:14. 16. John 14:6.

WILL YOU BAN THE BIBLE?

The Bible has been with us, for a very long time.
Read by countless millions, helped them out just fine.
Truths learned by many, but also many doubt.
A few more generations, when more of us die out,
Those who read the Bible, may well be a rare breed.
Please don't ban the Bible, on what then would I feed.

It's the most popular book and most read of all time.
Without exaggeration, it's the best read book of mine.
Although there are some who, its truths have not yet heard.
Some have tried to ban it, but can't destroy God's Word.
To be without the Bible my heart would really bleed.
Please don't ban the Bible, on what then would I feed.

People in this world, have suffered and been killed.
For reading their Bibles and becoming Spirit filled.
It tells us how to live our lives, how to love others as well,
How to care for our neighbours, who into hard times fell.
So to those in authority, I now would beg and plead.
Please don't ban the Bible, on what then would I feed.

Though we wrestle with it, for it isn't always clear,
Some don't want to understand, preferring just to sneer.
It can both provide us comfort and make uncomfortable.
It may challenge our lives, and make our spirits full.
For though God walks beside us, His Word we always need.
So, please don't ban the Bible, on what then would I feed.

WISDOM

If you could have one wish, I wonder what it would be.
Would it be worldly riches, or of more abstract quality?
You might wish to have knowledge, of all there is to know.
It's said the more you have, the more your power grows.
And if you wield your power, it will increase your wealth.
Would you use it to help others, or just to help yourself?
But riches, power and knowledge, are really not the prize.	1
Much higher and greater value, is the gift of being wise.	2

How does wisdom come about, just where can it be found?	3
Does it come to us, if we gather knowledge most profound?
Or perhaps with experience, it will then materialise.
If we live to a ripe old age, then would we be wise?
None of these suggestions, have proven to be true.
So if you seek wisdom, what is it you must do?
How do we define wisdom, what does it mean to be wise?
Is it wealth of knowledge or how knowledge then applies?

True wisdom, like grace, doesn't come to ordinary man.	4
Nor does it naturally grow for by God's Spirit it began.	5
Genuine wisdom starts with a real respect for the Lord.	6
And respecting Jesus means we must honour His holy Word.
Wisdom offers her treasures to those who pause and ask.	7
A truly abundant life awaits, in happiness they will bask.	8
Solomon asked God to give him an understanding mind,	9
To discern between good and evil, so God to him was kind.

God was very pleased with him, he did not ask for gain,
For victory over enemies, long life, or his own fame.
God not only gave Solomon what he had asked Him for,
He also gave him riches, honour and ever so much more.   10
That we can also do the same, may come as a surprise.
God offers us a free gift if we seek Him, to be wise.   11
The Apostle James said if any of us, does wisdom lack.
Ask our generous God to put us on a better track.

True wisdom is first hearing and then obeying God's Word.   12
But the wisdom of the natural man will say that is absurd.   13
Human reason and understanding believes the devil's lies.   14
Understanding truth, needs the Heavenly wisdom of the wise.   15
The truth is to hear the Word, and then the Word obey,   16
To find life's ultimate meaning this can be the only way.   17
When the storms of life assault, more solid will we stand.   18
He holds us firmly in His grip, we're covered by His hand.   19

Jesus said a foolish man builds his house upon the sand.   20
When the storms beat upon it, the house just cannot stand.
A man who builds His house on rock, is the one who's wise.
When the storms beat upon it, they don't lead to its demise.
And we can choose to be like the wise or foolish man.   21
We can ask God for wisdom to understand His plan.   22
For humbly respecting God, is from where true wisdom springs.   23
Peace with God, happiness and eternal life it brings.   24

1. Prov. 4:7–8. 2. 1 Sam. 15:22. 3. Prov. 4:5. 4. 1 Cor. 1:25. 5. Ps. 19:7. 6. Prov. 9:10.
7. Prov. 2:4, James 1:5. 8. John 10:10. 9. 2 Chron. 1:10–12. 10. Luke 11:31.
11. James 1:5. 12. Deut. 4:5–6, Sam. 15:22. 13. 1 Cor. 1:23–25, 3:19.
14. John 8:44, 2 Cor. 11:3–4. 15. 2 Thess. 2:10. 16. Prov. 8:32–36. 17. Eccl. 12:9–14.
18. Matt. 7:25. 19. Isaiah. 51:16, John 10:28. 20. Matt. 7:24–27.
21. Prov. 4:6–7, 2 Thess. 2:10. 22. James 1:5. 23. Prov. 9:10. 24. Prov. 3:13, 24:13–14.

WONDERFUL SAVIOUR
THE LION AND THE LAMB

How can anyone be seen as a lion and a gentle lamb,
A conqueror, yet humble, fitting into God's great plan?
Such was to be the message, which Jesus would unfold,
In the prophetic revelation, that to John He carefully told.

He is blessed who reads and listens to this true prophetic Word,
And takes to heart the message, of which he now has heard.
The faithful one, Jesus, who is ruler of all earth's Kings,
Was first to rise from death, now reveals to you these things.

A message from our God and from Jesus Christ His Son.
The One who *is* and also *was*, as well as who's *to come.*
The Apostle John in the Spirit, as it happened, the Lord's day,
Heard a voice behind him, drew his attention straight away.

When He turned around, for the One whose voice to see,
Fell down as dead before Him, in His presence feared to be.
Christ placed His hand upon him and said, "Don't be afraid."
So John to all the Lord's Words, his full attention paid.

He instructed John, that what he saw to write upon a scroll,
To churches in Asia Minor which were under His control.
He revealed what was to happen then, and at a future time.
His Words were clear and powerful, yet His temperament benign.

He moved on from this message to focus on God's throne.
Where many as they worshipped, threw at His feet, their crowns,
Saying, "You are worthy God, to receive glory, honour and power.
All things are made by Your will, and above them all You tower."   1

John saw in His hand a scroll with writing on both sides.
It was sealed with seven seals; then before his very eyes,
Appeared a mighty angel who asked, "Who can now reveal,
What the scroll contains, and is worthy to break its seal?"

John then wept and wept because no-one could be found,
In all of Heaven and earth; then the answer was profound.
A *being* told him not to weep, in Judah's tribe there is a Lion,
Who can open the scroll and seals, so the future will be fine.

John intently looked about him, thinking he'd see a Mighty Lion.
Instead he saw a Slain Lamb … that's all that He could find.
Then the Heavens sang a new song to the Lamb who had been slain,
"You're worthy to receive power, honour and glory to Your Name."

So the Lion of Judah is worthy, He is our mighty, powerful King.
Offered Himself before God's throne, a sacrificial Lamb to bring. 2
He's both the Lion and the Lamb, he's our King and our High Priest, 3
The humility of a Lamb, and the prowess of a Beast.

The Lamb upon the cross became the Lamb upon the throne.
Was resurrected and glorified with power to raise His own. 4
Tore apart the devil's kingdom, destroyed the power of sin and death. 5
Then arose a mighty conqueror, after drawing His last breath. 6

We may want a powerful God, who can destroy our enemy,
But His justice and His mercy are balanced perfectly. 7
God's power is like a Lamb slain, not like a roaring lion. 8
He willingly gave up His life, then rose to glory all sublime. 9

Jews looked for a Messiah, a Lion to conquer their enemy.   10
But they saw a weak and humble Lamb, who died upon a tree.   11
But as He hung upon that cross, did they see His glory there?
If they'd seen with eyes of faith, there'd be no reason to despair.   12

The slain Lamb who was taunted to express His awesome power,   13
Could have called a legion of angels who His enemies would devour.   14
The Lion could have shown great strength to certainly impress.
But the Lamb knew power in weakness as He triumphed over Death.   15

The resurrected, glorified Christ, seated now in God's throne room.   16
Those who trust in the Lamb slain, He will take home very soon.   17
Our sovereign King reigns over earth, the universe and Heaven rules.   18
Only One was worthy to open the scroll and to become Heaven's jewel.

Revelation Chs. 1–5. 1. Ps. 8:6, Eph. 1:22, 1 Cor. 15:25–26. 2. Isaiah 53:7, John 1:29, Heb. 9:12. 3. Heb. 1:3. 4. John 6:39–40. 5. Heb. 2:14-15. 6. Acts 2:24, Rev. 1:18. 7. Ps. 89:14, Matt 23:23, Romans 6:23. 8. Isaiah 53:7, 2 Cor. 12:9. 9. Phil 2:8–11. 10. Isaiah 2:4, 11:1–2, Micah 4:3. 11. Isaiah 53:7. 12. Matt. 27:42. 13. Luke 23:36–39. 14. Matt. 26:53. 15. 1 Cor. 1:28. 16. Heb. 8:1, 12:2, Rev. 3:21. 17. Matt. 24:30–33. 18. Col. 1:16.